"This wonderful collection of essays is an essential reading on the highly critical but less well understood dimension of the Sino-American strategic rivalry — their competition for technological dominance. A particular strength of these essays is their regional perspective on the implications of this contest for the small states of Asia."

Associate Professor Manjeet Singh Pardesi
Victoria University of Wellington, New Zealand

STRATEGIC CURRENTS

CHINA AND US COMPETITION FOR INFLUENCE

Strategic Currents

Print ISSN: 3029-1836
Online ISSN: 3029-1828

Series Editors:

Bernard F.W. Loo
S. Rajaratnam School of International Studies
Nanyang Technological University, Singapore

James Char
S. Rajaratnam School of International Studies
Nanyang Technological University, Singapore

Strategic Currents is an annual publication by the S. Rajaratnam School of International Studies. Each issue will be a collection of original essays by prominent scholars in the field of international security, centred on an issue or theme of emerging significance for regional and international security.

Published by World Scientific Publishing Co. Pte. Ltd.:

Strategic Currents: China and US Competition for Influence
    edited by Bernard F.W. Loo and James Char

Published by S. Rajaratnam School of International Studies,
Nanyang Technological University and Institute of Southeast Asian Studies,
National University of Singapore:

Strategic Currents: Issues in Human Security in Asia
    edited by Yang Razali Kassim

Strategic Currents: Emerging Trends in Southeast Asia
    edited by Yang Razali Kassim

Published by S. Rajaratnam School of International Studies,
Nanyang Technological University:

Strategic Currents: Marking the Transition to the S. Rajaratnam School of
International Studies
    edited by Yang Razali Kassim

STRATEGIC CURRENTS

CHINA AND US COMPETITION FOR INFLUENCE

Edited by

Bernard F.W. Loo

James Char

Published by

World Scientific Publishing Co. Pte. Ltd.

5 Toh Tuck Link, Singapore 596224

USA office: 27 Warren Street, Suite 401-402, Hackensack, NJ 07601

UK office: 57 Shelton Street, Covent Garden, London WC2H 9HE

National Library Board, Singapore Cataloguing in Publication Data
Name(s): Loo, Bernard Fook Weng, editor. | Char, James, editor.
Title: China and US competition for influence / edited by Bernard F.W. Loo, James Char.
Other Title(s): Strategic currents.
Description: Singapore : World Scientific Publishing Co. Pte. Ltd., [2024]
Identifier(s): ISBN 978-981-12-8807-4 (hardcover) | ISBN 978-981-12-8843-2
(paperback) | ISBN 978-981-12-8808-1 (ebook for institutions) | ISBN 978-981-12-8809-8
(ebook for individuals)
Subject(s): LCSH: Great powers--Foreign relations. | United States--Foreign relations--
China--21st century. | United States--Foreign relations--Southeast Asia--21st century. |
China--Foreign relations--United States--21st century. | China--Foreign relations--
Southeast Asia--21st century. | Southeast Asia--Foreign relations--United States--21st
century. | Southeast Asia--Foreign relations--China--21st century.
Classification: DDC 327.51073--dc23

British Library Cataloguing-in-Publication Data
A catalogue record for this book is available from the British Library.

Strategic Currents
STRATEGIC CURRENTS
China and US Competition for Inf uence

ISBN 978-981-12-8807-4 (hardcover)
ISBN 978-981-12-8843-2 (paperback)
ISBN 978-981-12-8808-1 (ebook for institutions)
ISBN 978-981-12-8809-8 (ebook for individuals)

For any available supplementary material, please visit
https://www.worldscientific.com/worldscibooks/10.1142/13726#t=suppl

Desk Editor: Kura Sunaina

Typeset by Stallion Press
Email: enquiries@stallionpress.com

Printed in Singapore

About the Editors

Bernard F. W. Loo is a Senior Fellow with the Military Studies Programme, and concurrently Coordinator of the Master of Science (Strategic Studies) Programme at the S. Rajaratnam School of International Studies (RSIS) at Nanyang Technological university (NTU), Singapore. He completed his doctoral studies at the Department of International Politics at the University of Wales, Aberystwyth in 2002. He is the author of *Medium Powers and Accidental Wars: A Study in Conventional Strategic Stability* (Edwin Mellen, 2005). His edited volume, *Military Transformation and Operations* (Routledge, 2009) was translated into complex Chinese for the Taiwanese military. His other publications have appeared in the *Journal of Strategic Studies, Contemporary Southeast Asia, NIDS Security Reports*, and *Taiwan Defense Affairs*. He is a regular commentator on defense matters, and his commentaries have appeared in *The Straits Times* (Singapore), *The Nation* (Thailand), and *The New Straits Times* (Malaysia).

 **James Char** is a Research Fellow with the China Programme at the S. Rajaratnam School of International Studies (RSIS) at Nanyang Technological University (NTU), Singapore. He is a specialist in Chinese domestic politics, civil-military relations in China, China's diplomatic strategies in the global south as well as the history of the Chinese Civil War. In addition to being a regular commentator on China's national and international politics in international media outlets, he has served as guest editor with top-tier peer-reviewed journals including *The China Quarterly*, *Journal of Strategic Studies*, and *Asian Security*. He is the editor of *Modernizing the People's Liberation Army: Aspiring to be a Global Military Power* (forthcoming, May 2024).

About the Contributors

Adrian Ang is a Research Fellow and Coordinator of the United States Programme in the Institute of Defence and Strategic Studies (IDSS) at S. Rajaratnam School of International Studies, Nanyang Technological University (NTU), Singapore. He holds a PhD in Political Science from the University of Missouri-Columbia, and his research interests include US foreign policy; American public opinion; political parties; elections, campaigns, and voting behaviour; and congressional politics.

Muhammad Faizal is a Research Fellow with the Regional Security Architecture Programme, Institute of Defence and Strategic Studies (IDSS) at the S. Rajaratnam School of International Studies (RSIS), Nanyang Technological University (NTU), Singapore. He holds a Master of Science (Strategic Studies) degree from RSIS, NTU and Bachelor of Business Administration (with Merit) from National University of Singapore. He has a research background in terrorism and geopolitical cyber threats. Prior to RSIS, he served many years in the Singapore Ministry of Home Affairs and National Security Coordination Secretariat where he headed teams in the roles of intelligence analysis, international relations, and national security analysis; achieving several commendation awards for operational and analysis efficiency. He also served a stint in the Ministry of Communications and Information where he focused on the intersection of digital security and geopolitics. His current research interests include the implications of diplomatic, informational, military, and cyber issues on regional security; entwinement of technology and geopolitics in the Indo-Pacific security architecture; as well as information/influence operations' and hybrid threats' challenges on regionalism.

Qi Haotian is an Assistant Professor at Peking University's School of International Studies, Senior Research Fellow at the Institute of International and Strategic Studies (IISS), Deputy Director of Center for International Security and Peace Studies (CISAP), and Secretary General of the Institute for Global Cooperation and Understanding (iGCU), Peking University (PKU). His research interests cut across four areas — Technological Transition and National Security, Military Strategy and Technology, Conflict Management, and Methodology of Social Sciences. His recent works focus on the impact and governance of military AI and influence of new technologies on interstate security relations and strategic stability. He teaches courses on International Security, Military Science, Game Theory, and International Public Policy.

Sarah Teo is an Assistant Professor in the Regional Security Architecture Programme and Deputy Coordinator of the MSc (International Relations) Programme at the S. Rajaratnam School of International Studies (RSIS), Nanyang Technological University (NTU), Singapore. Her research interests include multilateral security and defence cooperation in ASEAN and the Asia Pacific, middle powers in the Asia Pacific, as well as power in international relations. Her latest book is *Middle Powers in Asia Pacific Multilateralism: A Differential Framework* (Bristol University Press, 2023). She is the co-author of *Security Strategies of Middle Powers in the Asia Pacific* (Melbourne University

Publishing, 2018) and co-editor of *Minilateralism in the Indo-Pacific: The Quadrilateral Security Dialogue, Lancang-Mekong Cooperation Mechanism, and ASEAN* (Routledge, 2020). Her articles have also been published in peer-reviewed journals such as *International Theory, The Pacific Review*, and *Asia Policy*, edited volumes, as well as various commentary platforms. She has a PhD from the University of Sydney and MSc (International Relations) from RSIS.

Contents

CHAPTER 1

Introduction: Technology Competition Between China and the United States: Problems, Prospects, and Challenges

Bernard F. W. Loo and James Char

The growing contestations between the People's Republic of China (PRC, henceforth China) and the United States of America (henceforth the US) now span a range of dimensions, including the more traditional military, diplomatic, economic, and soft power realms. That the US–China relationship has now become the single most consequential Great Power competition confronting international politics in the 21st century is not in doubt. In view of what appears to be an emerging power transition between the global hegemon and the Asian giant, this Great Power dynamic has been characterised by American scholar Graham Allison as a potential Thucydides Trap.[1] Adding to this debate, other scholars have called

---

[1] Graham Allison, *Destined for War: Can America and China Avoid the Thucydides Trap?* (Houghton Mifflin Harcourt, 2017).

this US–China relationship a new Cold War,[2] although some continue to resist such labels.[3] Much, nevertheless, has been speculated about the possibility of a military conflict between China and the US, as a consequence. The Great Power dynamic of the 20th century mostly took on the unidimensional character of the Cold War between the former Soviet Union and the US, which had its diplomatic dimensions but was manifested to a large extent in a thermonuclear arms race. As it was, the Soviet Union's inability to compete with the US — both technologically and economically — led Australian scholar Paul Dibb to famously classify the Soviet Union as an "incomplete superpower".[4] In stark contrast to the late 20th century's Cold War adversaries, the current Great Power contest between China and the US is multifaceted, and both states are competing as peers, or at least near-peers, across a range of domains. Crucially, unlike the situation in the Cold War, Beijing and Washington are conjoined economically, with the trade and monetary exchanges between them involving a myriad of manufacturing industries and their consumer markets.

---

[2] See, for instance: Hal Brands and John Lewis Gaddis, "The new cold war: America, China, and the echoes of history", *Foreign Affairs* 100 (2021): 10–21; Avery Goldstein, "US-China Rivalry in the 21st Century: Déjà vu and Cold War II", *China International Strategy Review* 2 (2020): 48–62; Michael McFaul, "Cold War Lessons and Fallacies for US-China Relations Today", *Washington Quarterly* 43, no. 4 (2022): 7–39; Seth Schindler, Jessica DiCarlo and Dinesh Paudel, "The new cold war and the rise of the 21st-century infrastructure state", *Transactions of the Institute of British Geographers* 47, no. 2 (2022): 331–346; Yang Yao, "The New Cold War: America's new approach to Sino-American relations", *China International Strategy Review* 3 (2021): 20–33.

[3] See, for instance: Li Xing and Raul Bernal-Meza, "China-US rivalry: A new cold war or capitalism's intra-core competition?" *Revista Brasileira de Política Internacional* 64 (2021): 1–20, doi.org/10.1590/0034-7329202100110; Minghao Zhao, "Is a new cold war inevitable? Chinese perspectives on US–China strategic competition", *Chinese Journal of International Politics* 12, no. 3 (2019): 371–394, doi.org/10.1093/cjip/poz010.

[4] Paul Dibb, *The Soviet Union: The Incomplete Superpower* (University of Illinois Press, 1986).

In the military arena, this growing competition is best manifested in both Great Powers' respective defence budgets.[5] In 1990, China's defence budget (US$23 billion) consumed 2.5% of the country's gross domestic product (GDP), whereas the US defence budget (US$674 billion) took up 5.6% of the US GDP. By 2021, China's defence budget (US$297 billion) was reported to be 1.7% of its GDP, while the US defence budget (US$811 billion) was 3.6% of the American GDP. But, these figures alone do not convey the entire military picture, since the Chinese People's Liberation Army (PLA) has similarly expanded significantly in that same period: from a military "widely dismissed as a 'junkyard army'... saddled with outdated equipment [and] also hamstrung by problems with personnel quality, poor training, and the distractions and massive corruption"[6] to one that is "clearly becoming an increasingly professional and capable fighting force".[7]

In 2020, the Chinese naval fleet comprised 4 ballistic missile submarines, 7 nuclear-powered attack submarines, and 43 principal surface combatants (aircraft carriers, cruisers, and destroyers). By 2030, China's fleet will grow further to 8 ballistic missile submarines, 13 nuclear-powered attack submarines, and 65 principal surface combatants (of which 5 are likely to be aircraft carriers). Even if some doubts continue to linger regarding the combat quality of its aircraft

---

[5]   All data for Chinese and US defence spending come from the Stockholm International Peace Research Institute (SIPRI) Military Expenditure Database, https://milex.sipri.org/sipri. Figures are expressed in constant 2021 US dollars.

[6]   Michael S. Chase *et al.*, *China's Incomplete Military Transformation: Assessing the Weaknesses of the People's Liberation Army (PLA)* (Santa Monica, CA: RAND Corporation, 2015), p. 14.

[7]   *Ibid.*, p. 16.

carriers,[8] the Chinese military today ought to be recognised as an increasingly sophisticated armed force. At the same time, the PLA has been modernising its intercontinental ballistic missiles, of which the solid-fuelled Dongfeng (DF)-41 has an estimated circular error probability (that is, its accuracy) of 100 metres, representing a significant improvement on older Chinese ballistic missiles.[9] One study suggested that as early as 2017, the Chinese may already have gained the upper hand against the US in specific wartime scenarios, such as attacks on US air bases and the suppression of American surface combatants.[10]

The competition between these two Great Powers also takes place in the diplomatic realm. In that regard, and to borrow a phrase from the popular book, *How to Win Friends and Influence People*, China has made some gains in this sphere as part of its contestations to challenge the US-led global order. Indeed, the international influence Beijing now wields following four decades of economic liberalisation — without having to succumb to western pressures to politically reform — continues to hold allure for developing nations around the world. By offering a model that is both non-western and non-democratic for others still in the throes of development, China has been working to

---

[8] John Grady, "China's Navy could have 5 aircraft carriers, 10 Ballistic Missile Subs by 2030 says CSBA Report", *USNI News*, 18 August 2022, https://news.usni.org/2022/08/18/chinas-navy-could-have-5-aircraft-carriers-10-ballistic-missile-subs-by-2030-says-csba-report. On doubts regarding the quality of China's carriers, see, for instance: Greg Torode, Eduardo Baptista and Tim Kelly, "China's aircraft carriers play 'theatrical' role but pose little threat yet", *Reuters*, 5 May 2023, www.reuters.com/world/chinas-aircraft-carriers-play-theatrical-role-pose-little-threat-yet-2023-05-05/.

[9] Fiona S. Cunningham, "The unknowns about China's nuclear modernization", *Arms Control Association*, June 2023, www.armscontrol.org/act/2023-06/features/unknowns-about-chinas-nuclear-modernization-program.

[10] RAND Corporation, *Tallying the US-China Military Scorecard: Relative Capability and Balance of Power, 1996–2017*, RR-392-AF (Santa Monica, CA: RAND Corporation, 2015), pp. 1–4.

subvert the extant US-led order via a policy bestriding liberalist and constructivist platforms for realist ends. As part of its efforts to vie for global leadership, China's engagement with countries in the global south in particular has become more prominent in the wake of the COVID-19 pandemic as well as Russia's invasion of Ukraine. As a means of balancing against Washington's global preponderance, China's self-identification with other emerging economies, in addition to its drawing of institutional support from the global south, has recently been reinvigorated after the pandemic-induced hiatus as Beijing continues to translate its economic clout into a stronger political, diplomatic, and military presence *globally*.

Now a decade since its announcement in 2013, the Belt and Road Initiative (BRI) is the centrepiece of President Xi Jinping's diplomatic strategy, consisting of the "Silk Road Economic Belt" (an overland network of road and rail from China to Europe) and the "21st Century Maritime Silk Road" (comprising the sea routes through the Indo-Pacific via Southeast Asia, South Asia, and towards Africa and the Middle East).[11] Although some of its signatories have derived tangible economic benefits, this Chinese project has met with setbacks in other cases given how Beijing has had to spend equally vast sums of money to bail out countries struggling with their BRI debts[12] — not to mention the previous breakdown in global trade amidst the earliest phase of the pandemic. Additionally, the initiative continues to be plagued by reservations over the transparency and sustainability of its commodity-backed debt financing, inviting accusations that Beijing has strategically been exploiting host countries by saddling them with

---

[11] For a concise background, see Daniel Yergin, *The New Map: Energy, Climate, and the Clash of Nations* (Penguin Press, 2020), pp. 170–181.

[12] Amy Hawkins, "China woos global south and embraces Putin at belt and road Beijing summit", *The Guardian*, 16 October 2023.

"debt traps".[13] The BRI has been condemned even by some foreign communities supposedly served by Chinese investments, as can be seen in the example of terrorist attacks on Chinese nationals in the restive Balochistan region of Pakistan.[14] Most damagingly perhaps, the emergence of COVID-19 put a dent on the BRI as many related infrastructure projects were placed on hold, with as much as 20% of its programmes "seriously affected" in mid-2020.[15] Thus, even if Chinese officialdom recently touted BRI's contributions to "global connectivity, peace and prosperity",[16] its actual effect in boosting global development remains up for debate. Of late, the announcement of a new Global Development Initiative (GDI) in September 2021 also means the BRI could yet become subsumed under this more expansive framework.

Given the heftier economic resources at President Xi's disposal than at any other time in the PRC's history, China's international behaviour has similarly undergone major change. Even as the earlier "Wolf Warrior" diplomacy appears to have been abandoned for now, an emergent reorientation in China's approach to international relations — from "development" to "security" — has become apparent, with Chinese officials now touting their leader's Global Security Initiative

---

[13] Deborah Brautigam and Meg Rithmire, "The Chinese "debt trap" is a Myth", *The Atlantic*, 6 February 2021, www.theatlantic.com/international/archive/2021/02/china-debt-trap-diplomacy/617953/.

[14] Maham Hameed, "The politics of the China–Pakistan economic corridor", *Palgrave Communications* 4, no. 64 (2018): 1–10; and Adnan Aamir, "China wants own security company to protect assets in Pakistan", *Nikkei Asia*, 28 June 2022, https://asia.nikkei.com/Politics/International-relations/China-wants-own-security-company-to-protect-assets-in-Pakistan.

[15] Rene Zou, "Assessing the impact of Covid-19 on the belt and road initiative", Hong Kong Trade Development Council (HKTDC), 28 September 2020.

[16] Li Xuanmin and Qi Xijia, "BRI turns vision into action: White paper", *Global Times*, 10 October 2023.

(GSI) and the nebulous concept of "indivisible security" as an alternative to the US-led order. Running in parallel to the GDI and the Global Civilization Initiative (GCI), the new security concept incorporates the right to safeguard one's legitimate security interests, i.e., that no country's security should be built at the expense of others' security. Accordingly, Beijing could potentially seize the moral high ground should it decide to retaliate against US military activities that run counter to Chinese interests.

In light of the circumspection with which China eyes the world's top-ranked power, however, the effects of the GSI on actual Chinese policy have so far been mostly rhetorical. Just as Moscow has blamed the West and attributed the war in Ukraine to the expansion of the North Atlantic Treaty Organization (NATO), Beijing can be expected to continue agitating for the developing world to oppose so-called "US-led blocs" as it persists with accusing Washington of fomenting global conflicts and tensions.[17] Not unimportantly, it remains unclear whether the idea will receive the same level of institutional support domestically or be as well received outside China as the economically focused BRI. Especially on the latter, the reputational cost resultant from Beijing's association with Moscow in the aftermath of Russia's 2022 invasion of Ukraine may have already compromised the appeal of the GSI.[18]

As Beijing pursues the securitisation of its growing interests abroad while safeguarding its domestic socio-economic stability, it has maintained its efforts to garner multilateral, institutional support from the developing world to balance against the US. As a response to what

---

[17] Kathrin Hille, "China builds coalition to counter America's 'Barbaric and Bloody' leadership", *Financial Times*, 27 May 2020.

[18] *Reuters*, "U.S. says China continues to 'parrot' some Russian security concepts", *Reuters*, 22 April 2022.

the Chinese Communist Party (CCP) leadership perceives as Washington's containment policies, the party's armed wing, the PLA, has been playing a more visible role as a foreign policy instrument in Beijing's struggle for global hegemony. Concomitantly, as countries that had already signed up to China's ambitious infrastructure and investment plans resume their engagements after the COVID-19 pandemic, a number of strategically located developing countries have become the new focal point of Chinese affection as part of the PLA's putative "Project 141" initiative, which seeks to establish 5 overseas bases and 10 logistics support facilities by the year 2030.[19] Perhaps unsurprisingly, China has been observed to be focusing on extending its strategic depth from the western Pacific across the Indian Ocean and towards Africa via its diplomatic engagements in the global south. As manifested in the Chinese-brokered Saudi Arabia–Iran peace deal, the US has effectively been put on notice regarding Beijing's vision of an alternative global security order.

Further afield, neither the western Pacific nor Latin America has been neglected in Chinese strategic planning. Taking the Solomon Islands as an example, that same desire for securing overseas facilities likely also underpins Beijing's recent courtship of the Pacific Islands in a bid to bind them to a multilateral arrangement guaranteeing their security cooperation.[20] While the competition between Beijing and the

---

[19] John Hudson, Ellen Nakashima and Liz Sly, "Buildup resumed at suspected Chinese military site in UAE, leak says", *The Washington Post*, 26 April 2023, www.washingtonpost.com/national-security/2023/04/26/chinese-military-base-uae/. See also, Paul Nantulya, "Considerations for a prospective new Chinese Naval Base in Africa", Africa Center for strategic studies, 12 May 2022, https://africacenter.org/spotlight/considerations-prospective-chinese-naval-base-africa/.

[20] Kate Lyons and Dorothy Wickham, "The deal that shocked the world: Inside China-Solomons security pact", *The Guardian*, 20 April 2022, www.theguardian.com/world/2022/apr/20/the-deal-that-shocked-the-world-inside-the-china-solomons-security-pact.

western countries to win influence over the Pacific Islands has only recently come under the international spotlight, China has already secured a number of security pacts in Latin America this past decade. There, Beijing has invested in the region's space sector and signed into agreement arms deals with and the provision of military training to countries such as Venezuela, Cuba, and Bolivia.[21] Not unlike criticism that China's "string of pearls" across the Indian Ocean is a covert attempt to establish dual-use ports in the waters between the Straits of Malacca and the Gulf of Aden, Beijing's global economic and military outreach cannot be easily disaggregated. Since the late 2010s, China's influence over the region has also been reinforced as its economic strategy in the region has shifted from extending loans to making direct investments. Unlike their European counterparts, many Latin American economies have, in return, stepped up efforts to attract Chinese capital into their renewable energy sector, such as lithium development. Unlike the US and its western allies, countries in the region continue to show a desire for closer economic ties with Beijing — rather than endorse Washington's "friendshoring" approach vis-à-vis China.[22]

Increasingly, American efforts citing national security concerns to prevent advanced semiconductors from falling into the hands of Chinese tech companies have also been compromised. This ban extends to the design of these chips and the manufacturing equipment required to produce them, as well as those components used in the manufacturing equipment originating from the US. This last clause means that the sanctions apply not only to high-tech goods exported by US companies

21 Diana Roy, "China's growing influence in Latin America", *Backgrounder, Council on Foreign Relations,* Accessed 9 February 2023, www.cfr.org/backgrounder/china-influence-latin-america-argentina-brazil-venezuela-security-energy-bri.

22 Ryota Takahashi, *Analysis of the Theory that Latin America is Turning into 'China's Backyard' and the Outlook for the Future,* MGSSI Monthly Report (Tokyo, Japan: Mitsui & Co., Global Strategic Studies Institute, 2023), pp. 1–6.

but also those produced elsewhere using technologies licenced from American firms. Notwithstanding growing US export controls since the former Trump administration, the Chinese telecommunications behemoth Huawei was able to produce an advanced indigenous chip for its smartphone — with assistance from some Taiwanese firms. Clearly, much remains to be seen if and when Washington can perfect its policies in the face of a purported shadow network of chipmakers employed by Huawei to evade those sanctions,[23] and the US Commerce Department continues to be caught in a cat-and-mouse game with China, with the former needing to constantly update its policies.[24] While its techno-nationalist ambitions may have been stunted in the interim, Beijing continues to push back against the Biden administration just as Chinese companies continue their attempts at circumventing the export controls. At the Third Belt and Road Forum, China also declared its intent to challenge US leadership in this intensifying arena of contestation by advancing its own framework for artificial intelligence (AI) governance.[25]

This collection of essays refrains from addressing the thorny question of whether the current rivalry between China and the US constitutes a new Cold War. Rather, it focuses on what has perhaps become the most crucial aspect of this competition — the emerging technological contest between the two superpowers of our time, and its ramifications for small states in the Asia-Pacific region. In what originally started out as a trade war, this Great Power technological

---

[23] Bloomberg, "Key Taiwan Tech Firms Helping Huawei With China Chip Plants", *Bloomberg*, 3 October 2023.

[24] Josh Boak, "The commerce department updates its policies to stop China from getting advanced computer chips", *The Associated Press*, 17 October 2023.

[25] Dewey Sim, "Belt and road forum: China launches AI framework, urging equal rights and opportunities for all nations", *South China Morning Post*, 18 October 2023.

competition has since transformed into a competition for dominance in core information and communications technologies, in particular 5G telecommunications and AI, as well as advanced semiconductor chips, which underpin these technologies. As already mentioned, Washington's recent decision to pass new legislation to restrict Beijing's access to semiconductor chips — a key vulnerability in China's technological capabilities — can be understood through the lens of the incumbent hegemon's desire to prevent the rising power from usurping its "top-dog" status.

Importantly, what then are the ramifications of this intensifying technological contest between the two superpowers, especially for small states in the region that, like Singapore, seek to maintain diplomatic, economic, and strategic evenhandedness in their relations with both Beijing and Washington? The contributions in this volume serve to provide some answers. More specifically, they examine the following issues:

- Impact on trade between these states and the PRC and the US, and the long-term ramifications of the US restrictions;
- Impact on the technological ambitions of small states as well as the new challenges to global security and governance with respect to the potential threats to one's national security interests in the cyber and space domains;
- Impact on the ability of small states to maintain a strategic equidistance between both superpowers, and in particular these states' strategic autonomy to chart their respective diplomatic paths;
- How small states can help bring the major players to the table to formulate new mechanisms to prevent the actions of the PRC and the US from escalating into misadventures in the cyber and space realms; and

- In the nightmare scenario of the extant competition deteriorating into armed conflict between the two superpowers, what some of those choices and traps confronting small states might be.

The answers to these puzzles, we suggest, will allow us to reflect on the current regional security situation in the Asia-Pacific region and beyond, as well as serve to illuminate other lesser discussed issues in the study of the world's most significant bilateral relationship at present. First, given the advent of new technologies in the 21st century as the rivalry between the US and China expands and intensifies, it is pertinent to assess this emerging but potentially game-changing aspect of the Great Power competition. Second, in light of the deployment of novel military technologies in the Russia–Ukraine war as well as the crippling techno-economic sanctions imposed by the US and the West on Moscow, what concrete lessons has Beijing drawn to future-proof itself against similar embargoes in the unlikely event of a future contingency over the Taiwan Strait?

In the first chapter, Qi Haotian provides a Chinese perspective on the technological competition, and the challenges and opportunities this Great Power competition poses to smaller powers. Qi argues that this contest stems from a belief across US national security circles that these technologies possess "transformative potential" that will have significant implications for US national security interests. Washington, as Qi argues, seeks to maintain its leadership position and, as a consequence, perceives the need to prevent Beijing from challenging its dominance in cutting-edge technologies by curtailing "China's access to these technologies, products, and future developmental opportunities". For other third-party states, Qi suggests that they will have to "grapple with numerous questions simultaneously, including how to safeguard their national interests in a landscape marked by global economic and market uncertainties" and will also have to "decide whether to align with either of the two major powers, how to navigate political and economic tensions effectively, and how to transcend the bilateral discord and lay the groundwork for enduring and robust future development". In this regard, Qi anticipates a potentially constructive role for the states of the Association of Southeast Asian Nations (ASEAN). As Qi argues, ASEAN will be able to "contribute to the establishment of a dynamic equilibrium within future technopolitics", and in so doing, play a significant positive role in the "evolving landscape" at the "intersection of geopolitics and technopolitics".

Next, Adrian Ang addresses the issue of US aims and interests in what he depicts as an "increasingly acrimonious strategic rivalry" between the two superpowers of our time. Ang argues that the US perceives this rivalry as stemming from the increasingly fuzzy lines between the public and private spheres in China. Accordingly, US officials are "especially concerned by the blurring of lines between the Chinese party-state and the private sphere occurring under the concept of Military–Civil Fusion (MCF), which seeks to break down barriers to create stronger linkages between China's civilian economy and its defence industrial base". At present, China continues to suffer from a particular weakness, namely, its dependence on US companies as well as firms of the other US allies for the supply of advanced semiconductors. China, as such, is "highly vulnerable to being cut off from the supply of advanced semiconductors and being prevented from indigenising advanced chipmaking capabilities, thereby sustaining China's dependence on and vulnerability to the democracies". This US policy, which started under the Trump administration, has been further enhanced under the present Biden administration, which has banned the export of AI chips and semiconductor manufacturing technologies and equipment to China. Furthermore, the incumbent global technological leader has sought to restrict US investments in semiconductors, quantum information technologies, and AI.

Finally, Muhammad Faizal and Sarah Teo focus on ASEAN digital transformation efforts, and how this US–China competition could impact Southeast Asia. The authors argue that this technological competition presents the various ASEAN states with both opportunities and challenges. ASEAN's traditional policy — which they describe as "Don't make us choose" — has been, and will continue to be, challenged, even as individual ASEAN states appear to be profiting from this Great Power contest. Nevertheless, this Sino-US tussle for influence has led to the bifurcation of digital standards in the region. Laos, for instance, is dependent on Huawei for its infrastructure-building initiatives and is thus likely to be "locked in" to Chinese information and communications technologies, while some other ASEAN states remain aligned with US digital technologies and standards. What this means in the long term is that efforts in the regional harmonisation of these standards and their attendant legal regimes will face uncertainty. While individual ASEAN states have expressed concerns about this technological competition — with Singapore's Foreign Minister Vivian Balakrishnan depicting this phenomenon as a form of techno-nationalism — Faizal and Teo argue that ASEAN states will "continue their digitalisation policies based on the principles of political neutrality and economic pragmatism while concomitantly leveraging diplomatic fora to dissuade China and the US from weaponising their influence over technology".

Put together, these papers enable us to make better sense of the lesser-known aspects in this new arena of Great Power contest, and more importantly, provide a glimpse into the longer-term prospects for

Singapore and other small states to play a meaningful role in maintaining peace and stability in the region and beyond. Given that sufficient developments have taken place in the years since the earlier Trump-era trade sanctions to contain China's rise, there could not be a timelier endeavour to assess how this state of affairs regarding the nexus between security and technology has begun to play out in the ongoing Great Power struggle between China and the US.

https://doi.org/10.1142/9789811288081_0002

CHAPTER 2

Beyond US–China Competition: ASEAN at Technopolitical Intersection

Qi Haotian

Emerging high-end technologies play a crucial role in both the current global economy and the future progress of mankind. From an industrial perspective, these technologies have catalysed areas that generate annual sales amounting to trillions of US dollars. On the fundamental research front, the pioneering breakthroughs in these advanced domains determine our capacity to tackle impending grand challenges and uncertainties. The intricate and multifaceted supply chains of tech-enabled sectors often involve intricate processes and intricate supplier–customer relationships. In particular, the two countries arguably with the most significant prowess in numerous technological fields, the United States and China, grapple with a complex and strained relationship.

Current US policies concerning China's technological advancement reflect a belief in the transformative potential of new technologies and their implications for national security. By erecting barriers that prevent China from accessing advanced technologies and products, the United

States aims to assert its dominance as the singular leader in advanced technologies.[1] For instance, within the semiconductor industry, the United States maintains superiority in design and software, limiting China's entry to cutting-edge technology. In response, China actively seeks to bolster its indigenous capabilities. This situation has led to mounting concerns regarding the excessive securitisation and weaponisation of interdependence between the two nations. Both countries fear that the historical patterns of their bilateral relationship and their respective positions within global innovation and value chains could weaken due to their previously established economic and technological ties.

The competitive dynamics and even rivalry in technological development between the US and China have evolved into a nuanced game. The US seeks to uphold its leadership in foundational technologies by employing diverse measures to curtail China's access to existing high-end technology, products, and future developmental opportunities. Both nations are now in the process of delineating distinct spheres of influence, encompassing varying technological standards such as 5G, artificial intelligence (AI), and quantum computing. The nature of this relationship defies a simple characterisation as an offense–defence or action–reaction pattern.

Amidst the competition and rivalry between the US and China, third-party nations find themselves confronted with intricate challenges and multifaceted opportunities. They must grapple with numerous questions simultaneously, including how to safeguard their national interests in a landscape marked by global economic and market

---

[1] Emily Benson, Japhet Quitzon, and William Alan Reinsch, "Securing semiconductor supply chains in the Indo-Pacific economic framework for prosperity", *CSIS*, 30 May 2023, https://csis-website-prod.s3.amazonaws.com/s3fs-public/2023-05/230530_Benson_SemiconductorSupplyChains.pdf?VersionId=SlbU7F4LQk82X5EHlx1Ffjr7j.3nbfiu.

uncertainties. Additionally, they must decide whether to align with either of the two major powers, how to navigate political and economic tensions effectively, and how to transcend the bilateral discord and lay the groundwork for enduring and robust future development.

The countries within the Association of Southeast Asian Nations (ASEAN) occupy a distinctive and intricate position in this grand game of geopolitics and technopolitics. They are confronted with a range of distinct challenges while simultaneously encountering novel prospects. Beyond the role of mitigating the bilateral competition and tensions between Washington and Beijing, ASEAN member countries are also strategically positioned to contribute to the establishment of a dynamic equilibrium within future technopolitics. By doing so, they can pave the way for constructive engagement at the intersection of geopolitics and technopolitics, positioning themselves as a formidable force in this evolving landscape.

Technological Competition and Rivalry

The realm of high-end technology development has remained an arena of escalating tension and fierce competition between the United States and China in recent times. If we define "decoupling" as the process of diminishing mutual interdependence across various sectors, encompassing trade, investment, and technology, it is evident that such a decoupling has indeed transpired between the two nations. The US has independently taken actions and rallied its allies to enforce export controls and diverse restrictions, aiming to curtail China's entry into domains like advanced semiconductor technology and supercomputing capabilities. In response, China is actively pursuing high-tech self-reliance and has undertaken political, financial, and economic measures. While the term decoupling may carry varying interpretations and implications, it is unmistakable that the ongoing technological and technopolitical competition and rivalry are becoming intertwined with geopolitical tensions, culminating in an increasingly uncertain and precarious global economic and developmental landscape.

It is essential to recognise that the process of decoupling is intricate and multifaceted, manifesting distinct trends across different domains. Numerous corporations and industries maintain connections with both the United States and China, and despite the existing tensions, collaborative efforts persist in technology development. Such collaborations remain pertinent and mutually advantageous. For instance, in addressing global challenges, such as climate change, pandemics, and space exploration, cooperative ventures foster innovation and facilitate shared knowledge. However, in contentious and competitive realms like telecommunications, a comprehensive decoupling has not yet materialised. For major transnational corporations, the interconnectedness of technology and markets is deemed too indispensable to forsake.

Nonetheless, the broader trajectory of high-tech interactions between the United States and China does not offer an abundance of grounds for optimism. A discernible trend has emerged, characterised by escalating endeavours on both sides to diminish their reliance on each other within several pivotal spheres encompassing research, supply chains, and fundamental scientific innovation. The competition and rivalry have extended to the frameworks governing safety and security, technological alliances, ideological perspectives on technology, as well as value and industrial chains. The influence of the mounting constraints imposed by the US on technological collaboration has been extended to other sectors, including banking, venture capital funding, and domestic matters such as public security governance, which increasingly hinges on advanced technologies. The trajectory of the US–China technological relationship exhibits dual dimensions, with bilateral and global implications.

Bilateral competition and rivalry

In terms of the bilateral dynamics, the backdrop of decoupling is underscored by a complex interplay of trade tensions, the securitisation of innovation, and its weaponisation. Ongoing trade disputes between the United States and China, characterised by tariffs and trade-related conflicts, have prompted a reevaluation of their technological interdependency and a heightened pursuit of self-sufficiency. Intrinsically linked to these tensions is the growing securitisation of technological advancements within both countries.

Consequently, concerns related to intellectual property theft, coerced technology transfers, and potential security vulnerabilities posed by Chinese technology entities have raised alarms within the United States and among its allies and partners. This has precipitated heightened scrutiny and tighter restrictions on technology transfers and collaborative endeavours with China, thereby engendering additional economic and innovation risks from the Chinese standpoint.

Both the United States and China have enacted export controls and sanctions targeting specific high-tech products and technologies, progressively transforming the technological, economic, and industrial relationship into an arena of contention and strategic influence. These measures have effectively endowed technological assets with a combative purpose, justified as safeguarding national interests and averting the potential proliferation of sensitive technologies to possible adversaries.

A case in point is the semiconductor policy under the Biden administration, which engenders differing interpretations in the two nations, leaving scant room for reconciliation. From the perspective of the US, this policy emerges as a response to concerns relating to national interests, security imperatives, and commercial as well as normative considerations. In contrast, China views this policy through a lens that leaves little doubt that the stringent performance thresholds for chips destined for China and the anticipated denial of export licences for chips exceeding such thresholds are aimed at curbing, and to some extent asphyxiating, China's access to advanced AI computing, chip design software, and semiconductor manufacturing equipment.

Global and structural trends

The ongoing shifts in global supply chains and the competition surrounding technological innovation have seemingly set the stage for an inevitable decoupling process. Factors such as the COVID-19 pandemic and geopolitical considerations have prompted both transnational and domestic companies worldwide to reevaluate their supply chain strategies. Some enterprises have pursued diversification of their sourcing away from China, driven by concerns over costs and uncertainties with political and economic implications.

Furthermore, the US and China are embroiled in a competitive race to achieve technological supremacy, particularly in domains such as AI, 5G, quantum computing, and biotechnology. This rivalry has fostered an environment where both nations are vigorously striving to independently lead in cutting-edge technologies.

It is important to underscore that the notion of decoupling was never confined solely to a bilateral matter between the US and China. The United States and its allies have undertaken measures to curtail collaboration with China in high-tech development. Government agencies and private corporations within the United States and allied nations may face limitations on engagement with Chinese counterparts or researchers concerning specific high-end chip projects, particularly those with potential applications in dual-use contexts.

In the pursuit of restricting China's access to and development of high-tech capabilities, and to gain a competitive edge, a myriad of strategies have been employed. Firstly, the US government has imposed export controls on select high-end technologies, equipment, and software, under the guise of averting the transfer of sensitive technologies with potential military or security applications. These controls necessitate companies, including non-American entities, to secure licences before exporting such technologies to China. In the high-end semiconductor industry, for instance, the US government has enforced stringent export controls on advanced semiconductor technologies and equipment, especially those with potential military implications. This encompasses technologies integral to the production of high-end chips, including extreme ultraviolet lithography machines and advanced manufacturing equipment.

Notably, in January 2023, a collaborative effort between the United States, the Netherlands, and Japan culminated in an agreement to collectively impose export controls on advanced semiconductor equipment.[2] Subsequently, the Dutch and Japanese governments followed suit by introducing new export controls on semiconductor technology in March 2023. Of particular significance, the Japanese Ministry of Economy, Trade, and Industry (METI) announced an

---

[2] Gregory C. Allen, Emily Benson, and Margot Putnam, "Japan and the Netherlands announce plans for new export controls on semiconductor equipment", *CSIS*, 10 April 2023, www.csis.org/analysis/japan-and-netherlands-announce-plans-new-export-controls-semiconductor-equipment.

amendment to the Foreign Exchange and Foreign Trade Act on 23 May 2023. This amendment incorporated 23 categories, including advanced chip manufacturing equipment, into the list of controlled export items, and came into effect on 23 July. These coordinated actions underscored a shift towards intensified geopolitics and technopolitics within the realm of global high-tech relations.

Nevertheless, the extent of collaboration by US allies to support their intertwined high-tech industrial policies vis-à-vis China remains to be seen. While the trend of reduced external linkage is evident and consistent, notable initiatives such as the US CHIPS and Science Act allow foreign-owned companies like IBM to receive US subsidies. Similarly, the European Union's European Chips Act aims to bolster the semiconductor ecosystem with reduced external dependencies.

Secondly, the United States has included specific high-tech Chinese companies on trade blacklists such as the Entity List. Inclusion on this list curtails their access to US technologies and components. In the realm of high-end semiconductors, for instance, the US Department of Commerce has added certain Chinese companies, including those active in the semiconductor sector, to the Entity List. This designation restricts the access of these entities to US technologies, components, and software, thereby limiting their capacity to engage in collaborative endeavours with US counterparts for high-end chip development.

Thirdly, the United States and its allies have intensified scrutiny over global supply chains within high-tech industries, with concerns centred on intellectual property theft and coerced technology transfers, particularly concerning Chinese involvement. Consequently, companies have adopted a more cautious and risk-averse stance when it comes to sharing proprietary high-end technologies with Chinese partners. Enhanced scrutiny measures have translated into heightened due diligence concerning companies engaged in the utilisation of specific manufacturing equipment and technologies, as well as the production of advanced high-end products. For instance, within the high-end semiconductor industry, the United States has escalated the scrutiny of investments originating from Chinese entities. The Committee on Foreign Investment in the United States (CFIUS) holds the authority to review and potentially block foreign investments that present national security risks, especially those related to critical technologies such as high-end chips.

Fourthly, some nations have implemented or contemplated restrictions on investments originating from China within the semiconductor industry, particularly in pivotal areas encompassing advanced chip manufacturing and design. Within the high-end semiconductor industry, the United States has released guidelines and imposed limitations on technology exports to China, specifically within the semiconductor sector. These guidelines are designed to thwart the transfer of technologies and equipment that could enhance China's semiconductor capabilities, particularly in sensitive domains.

Fifthly, the United States and its allies have exercised caution in sharing cutting-edge research and development knowledge with Chinese entities, especially in areas deemed sensitive from a national security perspective. Within the high-end semiconductor domain, research institutions and technology companies in the United States may be subject to restrictions on collaboration with Chinese counterparts in pioneering semiconductor research and development, particularly within sectors considered critical for national security. Both the United States and its allied nations have issued guidelines to their technology firms, augmenting export guidelines and outlining specific technologies and equipment that should not be exported or shared with Chinese entities without obtaining proper approvals.

Given the multifaceted implementation of these measures and the prospect of further actions, the US government is also of the opinion that China is poised to take exceptional measures to attain independence from current supply and value chains. This perspective potentially renders US policies and actions self-fulfilling prophecies. As the quest for super-technological prowess and leverage gradually transforms into an existential imperative, the structural rivalry with China assumes a zero-sum paradigm in the eyes of the United States. This shift in dynamics has led to widespread and intricate repercussions within the global landscape.

Global Implications of US–China Technology Relations

The ramifications of technological competition and rivalry between China and the US extend significantly to other nations worldwide, particularly middle powers and smaller countries. These implications span various domains, encompassing the global economy, technological advancement, geopolitics, and trade dynamics.

A majority of nations maintain robust economic connections with both China and the United States. As the process of decoupling unfolds, these countries encounter direct and indirect repercussions due to shifts in supply chains, alterations in trade patterns, and shifts in the dynamics of the global economy. The outcome for individual nations may involve seizing new manufacturing roles or grappling with adverse effects rooted in their dependence on exports to either China or the United States. The impact of this ongoing competition and rivalry is intricate and multifaceted.

Supply chain disruption

The unsettling state of technological relations between these two nations has precipitated disruptions within global supply chains. The process of decoupling technology has the potential to restrict the accessibility of critical high-tech components and products within the global marketplace. Nations reliant on both the US and China for advanced technology may encounter challenges in procuring vital components, thereby affecting industries such as telecommunications, consumer electronics, and automotive.

Numerous countries rely heavily on China for manufacturing and the integration of supply chains. As the process of decoupling advances, disruptions in the flow of goods and components reverberate across businesses and industries on a global scale. Nations significantly reliant on China as a manufacturing nucleus might be compelled to explore alternative sources, potentially yielding elevated costs and delays in production.

China's distinguished reputation as the "world's factory" is attributed to its extensive manufacturing capacities and integration within global supply chains. The progression of decoupling and its deepening ramifications can result in interruptions to the flow of goods, components, and technology between China and the United States, culminating in the fragmentation of supply chains. Companies, consequently, must seek alternative suppliers and manufacturing partners in other nations, potentially leading to delays and escalated costs. The endeavour to transition manufacturing operations to alternative countries could entail augmented production costs due to less streamlined processes and increased transportation expenditures. Mitigating risks linked to the decoupling process may necessitate the restructuring of supply chains, including the potential relocation of manufacturing facilities or the sourcing of components from diverse regions — an endeavour that is both resource-intensive and time-consuming.

Crucially, within certain pivotal sectors, diverse nations exhibit varying sentiments concerning the process of decoupling, given the extensive length and complexity of value and supply chains. For instance, the global semiconductor value chain is marked by intricate processes and intricate supplier–customer relationships. Notably, the United States leads in design and software, while Japanese, Taiwanese, German, and South Korean firms serve as principal suppliers of silicon wafers. Dominance in wafer fabrication and advanced packaging equipment is shared between the United States and Japan. Meanwhile, China boasts a considerable number of ATP facilities. The convergence of technopolitics and geopolitics adds an extra layer of complexity, influencing the choices made by distinct countries.

Technology access

The rivalry in technological prowess between China and the United States yields both positive and negative repercussions concerning technological access. If decoupling becomes a reality, other nations might experience constraints in accessing cutting-edge technologies and engaging in research collaborations. This scenario holds the potential to impede global technological progress and hinder cooperative endeavours within the realms of AI, 5G technology, and advanced manufacturing.

The competitive atmosphere fosters an environment of heightened protectionism and the erection of barriers to technological access. Both China and the United States may tighten export controls and restrict the transfer of crucial technologies to one another as well as to other nations. This approach carries the risk of constraining technological access and impeding collaborative innovation.

Competitive dynamics could escalate concerns regarding intellectual property theft and violations. Consequently, safeguarding intellectual property becomes imperative for corporations and governments, which occasionally curtails the cross-border sharing of technology and innovation.

However, some nations may strategically position themselves as alternative hubs for manufacturing and technology, capitalising on the evolving situation. These countries might attract investments and businesses aiming to diversify their supply chains away from both China and the United States.

Economic patterns

Supply chain disruptions stemming from the competitive rivalry can exert pressure on trade relations between nations. Tariffs and export restrictions could be imposed in response to the evolving landscape, triggering trade disputes and protectionist actions.

The process of decoupling simultaneously stimulates trade diversification. Third-party countries will seek to expand their trade relationships to mitigate risks stemming from technological decoupling. Enhanced partnerships with other nations might be forged to secure technology and goods that were previously obtained from either China or the United States.

Numerous multinational corporations boast intricate supply chains that span multiple countries. The process of decoupling could potentially disrupt their operations, introducing regulatory hurdles and instilling uncertainty concerning future investments. Technological decoupling may introduce uncertainties and risks within financial markets, particularly for companies with significant exposure to

US–China trade relations. Investors might recalibrate their strategies, leading to fluctuations in the global flow of investments. For instance, the US Bureau of Industry and Security's (BIS) 2022 announcement concerning export controls precipitated a decline in stock prices for Asian chip manufacturers, anticipated disturbances in supply chains, and prompted the scaling back of operations by foreign semiconductor equipment suppliers in China.[3]

The competitive dynamics at play can trigger economic shifts that impact countries reliant on the technological and industrial output of either China or the United States. As supply chains adapt and markets realign, nations may grapple with challenges or unearth opportunities contingent upon their trade and economic affiliations. Amidst these developments, calls for greater policy predictability and precision in targeting export controls have emerged. The implications are palpable for Western producers within a recalibrated global semiconductor ecosystem, influencing market shares and profitability.

Innovation and technological evolution

In the context of long-term innovation and technological cycles, the continuation of the decoupling process could potentially lead to the emergence of distinct technological standards and regulations within various regions. Should the trajectory of technological competition persist, both nations may forge their distinct technological standards and ecosystems, possibly resulting in parallel technologies lacking full

---

[3] Sujai Shivakumar, Charles Wessner, and Thomas Howell, "A seismic shift: The new US semiconductor export controls and the implications for US firms, allies, and innovation ecosystem", *CSIS*, 14 November 2022, https://csis-website-prod.s3.amazonaws.com/s3fs-public/publication/221114_Shivakumar__ExportControlImplications_v2.pdf?VersionId=1SyaKGTyhKCu0jkMw1ePtAkAPoSOw4f1.

compatibility.[4] This scenario has the potential to engender fragmentation within the global technology landscape, thereby complicating international collaboration, technology cooperation, and overall compatibility.

However, the intensity of competition can serve as a catalyst for substantial investments in research and development (R&D) by both countries. As they vie to surpass each other, significant technological breakthroughs may transpire across diverse fields, spanning AI, biotechnology, renewable energy, and telecommunications. The competitive milieu may fuel accelerated innovation, propelling one nation ahead in specific technologies. In their quest for competitive advantage, both countries might bypass antiquated technologies in favour of cutting-edge solutions, potentially benefiting other nations that adopt these advancements. Nevertheless, it remains highly likely that the escalating uncertainties and risks stemming from this competition might lead to reductions in research investments within both the public and private sectors.

Geopolitical and technopolitical dynamics

The implications of technological decoupling between China and the United States reverberate across global supply chains, presenting a landscape where potential winners and losers emerge across various industries and nations. Both companies and governments will need to adeptly navigate these transformative shifts to uphold efficient and resilient supply chain networks.

The decoupling process not only shapes US–China geopolitics but also exerts an impact on regional and global technopolitics. This

---

4   Justin Feng, "The costs of US–China semiconductor decoupling", *CSIS*, 25 May 2022, www.csis.org/blogs/new-perspectives-asia/costs-us-china-semiconductor-decoupling.

phenomenon could amplify pre-existing geopolitical tensions between these two nations, possibly triggering diplomatic and political strains on a global scale. Nations may find themselves under pressure to adopt a stance or manoeuvre through intricate relationships with these two superpowers. Some countries may strategically position themselves to leverage the evolving scenario, capitalising on potential opportunities. In the event that China and the United States impose export restrictions on one another, nations with fewer trade barriers could seize a competitive advantage within specific markets.

The geopolitical and technopolitical repercussions of US–China science and technology relations present a complex and multifaceted landscape for third-party nations. While certain countries have reaped benefits from the evolving industrial landscape, particularly within the semiconductor sector, they are also confronted with the challenge of navigating geopolitical tensions while safeguarding their economic interests. European corporations, for instance, are polarised in their responses to China's technological aspirations — some are bolstering their presence in China, while others are diversifying their operations. US export controls have introduced uncertainties for European entities, raising compliance complexities and the potential for disruptions within the semiconductor supply chain.[5] The European Union, with its distinct digital sovereignty and regulatory framework, grapples with its unique set of challenges vis-à-vis the United States.

Within Latin America, the landscape is similarly intricate, encompassing political, technological, diplomatic, economic, and personal considerations. In the context of 5G, for instance, while certain Latin American nations may have initially been inclined towards the

---

5   Antonia Hmaidi and Rebecca Arcesati, "Why Europe struggles with US export controls on China", *The Diplomat*, 27 December 2022, https://thediplomat.com/2022/12/why-europe-struggles-with-us-export-controls-on-china/.

highest bidder in the 5G discourse, their decisions were ultimately also shaped by geopolitical and diplomatic factors. Many nations faced the dilemma of striking a balance between ties with Beijing and Washington. Efforts to include monitoring mechanisms or negotiate financial support in return for limiting or banning Huawei's participation underscore the gravity of their decisions, which carry wide-ranging implications for the broader region.[6]

Navigating complexity in Asia: The case of South Korea

Within Asia, the landscape is notably intricate, with South Korea assuming a pivotal role in the unfolding narrative. The nation holds a vital position in the semiconductor production industry, with China serving as its primary trading partner for semiconductor chips. The semiconductor manufacturing sector holds critical importance for South Korea's economy, contributing to nearly 6% of its GDP, while memory chip exports alone accounted for 9% of total exports in 2022, with over 70% directed towards mainland China and Hong Kong.[7]

The imposition of US export controls on China raises pertinent concerns regarding South Korea's endorsement of these measures, given their potential impact on the nation's economic interests. The intricate nature of the semiconductor supply chain, coupled with South Korea's economic affiliations to both the United States and China, presents the nation with the formidable challenge of navigating the complex terrain of geopolitics and technopolitics.

---

[6]   Oliver Stuenkel, "Latin American governments Are caught in the middle of the US–China Tech War", *Foreign Policy*, 26 February 2021, https://foreignpolicy.com/2021/02/26/latin-america-united-states-china-5g-technology-war/.

[7]   Troy Stangarone, "China's ban of micron puts South Korea in the worst of both worlds", *The Diplomat*, 3 June 2023, https://thediplomat.com/2023/06/chinas-ban-of-micron-puts-south-korea-in-the-worst-of-both-worlds/.

South Korean semiconductor firms maintain substantial economic ties with China, with a significant proportion of DRAM (Dynamic Random Access Memory) and NAND (Not-And) chip production happening within Chinese facilities. The imperative set forth by Washington for Seoul to align with export controls, coupled with Beijing's reactions such as the ban on Micron's semiconductors in critical infrastructure, exemplifies the intricate position third-party nations may find themselves in.

The intricacies surrounding memory chip production — in South Korea led by Samsung, SK Hynix, and Micron — inevitably involve the country in this dispute, whether by design or by circumstance. As the United States urges Korean companies not to fill potential losses stemming from China's decision, South Korea is thrust into a complex predicament. Given their robust economic interests and production capabilities, Samsung and SK Hynix are poised to mitigate potential shortages resulting from the Micron ban.[8] However, industry downturns and surplus capacity introduce additional layers of complexity to their decision-making. More critically, from a political perspective, the South Korean government has indicated its disinclination to actively encourage firms to assume this role.

In conclusion, the dynamics of technological competition and rivalry between China and the United States hold the potential to catalyse substantial technological progress and innovation. Yet, they may also introduce an array of challenges concerning access, collaboration, economic stability, and resilience. As the world grapples with mounting uncertainties and risks stemming from this intense competition, a nuanced understanding of these multifaceted implications is imperative for all stakeholders involved.

---

[8] Stangarone, "China's Ban of Micron".

ASEAN at the Intersection of Geopolitics and Technopolitics

The ongoing technological competition and rivalry between the United States and China encompass a wide spectrum of sectors, including but not limited to the semiconductor industry, AI, 5G, biotechnology, quantum computation, and space exploration. These domains span both civilian and military realms, traversing the boundaries between fundamental sciences and applied technologies. Amidst this diverse landscape, three pivotal arenas emerge as profoundly influential, competitive, and, to some extent, "decoupled". These domains, characterised by their critical roles in the global economy and the intricate dynamics of US–China science and technology interactions, hold significant implications for third-party nations, particularly those of smaller scale such as the ASEAN countries. Positioned at the confluence of geopolitics and technopolitics, ASEAN countries are confronted with distinct challenges and opportunities.

Multifaceted impact

ASEAN occupies a pivotal position in both global and regional trade, serving as a vital partner for both the United States and China. Many ASEAN countries are integral players in the global trade and supply chain landscape, often acting as manufacturing hubs and suppliers of essential raw materials. The evolving technological dynamics between the United States and China exert multifaceted impacts on ASEAN countries.

The technological interplay between the United States and China reverberates within the region's trade dynamics, influencing the demand for ASEAN exports to these major players. Potential disruptions in their technological relations could precipitate shifts in the structures of supply chains.

Foreign direct investment (FDI) constitutes a significant component of ASEAN economies, attracting substantial contributions from both the United States and China. Sectors such as manufacturing, infrastructure, and technology often serve as recipients of this investment. The escalating technological competition between these superpowers can potentially recalibrate the nature and volume of investments within ASEAN, as companies reevaluate their strategies through the lens of trade and geopolitical considerations.

The technological decoupling between the United States and China manifests as a notable factor impacting ASEAN countries' access to critical technologies. These countries commonly rely on both nations for technology and innovation inputs, making restrictions on technology transfers a constraint to their ability to adopt advanced solutions across various industries.

Vietnam: A microcosm of challenges and opportunities

Within this context, the case of Vietnam features the challenges and opportunities emerging from the technological landscape. As a potential focal point for South Korean semiconductor manufacturers seeking alternative markets amidst sluggish demand in China, Vietnam has positioned itself as an attractive destination.[9] Its abundant low-cost labour force and proximity to the Chinese market have spurred global corporations, including South Korean entities, to establish manufacturing facilities within its borders. The US–China trade tensions have propelled

---

[9]   *Viet Nam News*, "VN attracts global semiconductor manufacturers", *Viet Nam News*, 19 July 2023, https://vietnamnews.vn/economy/1549956/vn-attracts-global-semiconductor-manufacturers.html.

investments in Vietnam's semiconductor sector. Nevertheless, the scarcity of skilled labour presents a significant hurdle to sustained growth.

Singapore, Malaysia, and Thailand: Caught amidst semiconductors' crossfire

Singapore, Malaysia, and Thailand, like Vietnam, find themselves ensnared in the midst of the US–China semiconductor rivalry. In the short term, they may stand to benefit from the trade war, as companies relocate their operations and actively solicit semiconductor investments to diversify the global supply chain.[10] Key semiconductor manufacturers are expanding their chipmaking capacities within these regions. The strategic positioning and policy framework of these nations enable them to evolve into dependable partners for US corporations striving to diversify their chip sources. However, the persisting uncertainty on the geopolitical front and potential supply chain disruptions may cast a shadow on the region's long-term access to advanced technology.

Navigating digital frontiers: ASEAN's pragmatic approach

In the realm of the global digital economy, both the United States and China wield significant influence. The ramifications of their technological interactions extend to the development of ASEAN's digital economy. In light of the intensifying competition and rivalry between

---

[10] James Guild, "Why US-China Rivalry might be good for Singapore's semiconductor industry", *The Diplomat*, 13 July 2021, https://thediplomat.com/2021/07/why-us-china-rivalry-might-be-good-for-singapores-semiconductor-industry/; Thamini Vijeyasingam, "US-China chip war escalation yet to rock Malaysia's boat", *Free Malaysia Today*, 11 April 2023, www.freemalaysiatoday.com/category/highlight/2023/04/11/us-china-chip-war-escalation-yet-to-rock-malaysias-boat/.

these superpowers, certain ASEAN countries might align themselves with one side or the other in terms of digital infrastructure, standards, and regulations. This geopolitical choice, influenced by destined geostrategic considerations and economic factors, potentially impacts ASEAN countries' efforts to chart their digital trajectory.

Yet, such an alignment raises intricate challenges, as differing technological and data regulations from the United States and China necessitate meticulous navigation. As these two giants set their individual standards, ASEAN countries may find themselves compelled to adopt measures ensuring compatibility with both systems or opt for an approach aligned with their distinct developmental goals.

The escalating technological competition between the United States and China heightens uncertainties and risks related to cybersecurity and data privacy for ASEAN countries. As these countries engage with technologies and digital platforms from both sides, safeguarding data protection and security emerges as a paramount concern.

In navigating the complex interplay of US–China technological rivalry, ASEAN countries espouse a pragmatic approach. While competition between the two giants extends beyond 5G into emerging domains like AI and cloud computing, Southeast Asian nations prioritise diversity within their 5G development endeavours. Notably, amidst pressures from the United States, ASEAN has adopted a nuanced equilibrium, evading a forced allegiance in the ongoing technological race.[11]

Southeast Asia's reliance on AI technologies imported from both the United States and China underscores the region's agency in selecting

---

[11] For instance, in the recent years, ASEAN and China issued quite a positive joint statement after the special session of ASEAN–China ministerial meeting on science, technology, and innovation on 14 December 2021. The two also signed and reiterated the need to deliver on the ASEAN–China Plan of Action on a Closer Partnership of Science, Technology, and Innovation for Future (ACPASTI) 2021–2025. For additional details on the joint statement, see https://most.gov.cn/kjbgz/202204/t20220422_180304.html.

technologies and negotiating favourable terms. However, this dependency poses challenges alongside short-term competitive advantages. The persistent reliance on AI technologies from these global titans may potentially undermine multilateralism and exert long-term ramifications on Southeast Asian nations.

Within the 5G landscape, ASEAN countries advocate for technological neutrality, empowering member states to designate their preferred technology providers for 5G networks. While the United States voices concerns over integrating Chinese 5G technology due to cybersecurity apprehensions, ASEAN countries endorse a multi-vendor approach, shielding against reliance on a single provider. This approach allows them to address cybersecurity concerns while bolstering their digital economy through capacity-building initiatives.

For instance, despite America's cautionary stance on Chinese equipment, most ASEAN member states have refrained from excluding major Chinese 5G providers, including Huawei, from their technological advancement. Embracing a multi-vendor strategy, some nations consider Huawei's cost-effective 5G solutions despite cybersecurity reservations. Meanwhile, European vendors such as Ericsson and Nokia have emerged as preferred choices for 5G networks in select Southeast Asian countries.

The multifaceted impact of US–China technological relations reverberates across the diverse ASEAN countries. The implications encompass both beneficial and challenging facets. In the immediate term, the US–China rivalry in Southeast Asia presents an opportunity to negotiate favourable terms and access a broader array of choices. However, in the longer trajectory, the divergence between Chinese and American technologies, standards, and norms could potentially herald a diminution of multilateralism. To address these complexities, ASEAN governments must meticulously weigh their options, strategically plan, and adeptly navigate the evolving global technology landscape.

ASEAN's Path Forward

ASEAN countries find themselves immersed in a complex and challenging environment. The region grapples with the increasing confluence of Chinese product and service providers, as well as the broader US–China competition. An illustrative example is the decision of major telecommunications providers across various ASEAN countries in 2020 to opt for European vendors over Huawei for their 5G networks due to US pressures. While several member states initially embraced Chinese technology and services, a shift is apparent as some countries and entities begin to recalibrate their collaboration with China. This shift, often echoed in US-supported rhetoric, portrays such collaboration as uncertain and unsafe.

Pragmatism: The guiding principle

However, pragmatism, rooted in practical considerations rather than political or ideological affiliations, remains the cornerstone of ASEAN's approach and its journey ahead. Striking a delicate equilibrium between competition and cooperation will prove essential to advancing technology for the region's betterment. ASEAN holds a distinctive position, capable not only of securing its interests but also of acting as a stabilising force amidst mounting tensions between the United States and China, contributing to both regional and global development.

ASEAN countries, each with its unique interests and inclinations, must exercise caution to avoid becoming ensnared in the US–China tech rivalry. They should endeavour to safeguard their digital economies while concurrently pursuing economic opportunities within the context of the Fourth Industrial Revolution (4IR). While the US–China tech rivalry casts its shadow on the agendas, ASEAN remains resolute in its commitment to digital development. Guided by a philosophy of neutrality and a development-oriented outlook, ASEAN possesses the capacity to adeptly navigate the intricacies of technological advancement, simultaneously upholding its reputation and credibility within the technology and innovation spheres.

ASEAN countries have the potential to act as catalysts for regional innovation and collaboration in response to the US–China technological competition. By fostering partnerships among local industries, universities, and research institutions, ASEAN can fortify its domestic and regional innovation capabilities.

ASEAN's pragmatic approach, characterised by technological neutrality and a multi-vendor orientation, proves more advantageous for the development of areas such as AI and 5G. This approach serves both national and regional interests, diverging from a complete alignment with either superpower. Preserving an open, equitable, and competitive market stands as a pivotal tenet for ASEAN's credibility and trustworthiness as the technological landscape evolves. As the dawn of the digital era unfolds, ASEAN countries must craft a unified strategy to safeguard their values and interests, while simultaneously assuming a unique position in maintaining a grand technopolitical ecosystem for the broader international community.[12] While astutely weighing the implications of the escalating tech rivalry and potential "arms race", ASEAN plays a vital role in preventing this competition from escalating into a full-fledged tech war.

---

[12] ASEAN has been preparing for and working on this for years, as exemplified in the ASEAN Plan of Action on Science, Technology, and Innovation (APASTI) 2016–2025.

Strategic navigation: A multifaceted approach

To deftly navigate the implications of the US–China technological rivalry, ASEAN countries might consider fortifying several strategies.

Firstly, diversifying trade partnerships beyond the United States and China is of paramount importance. Strengthening economic ties with alternative countries and regions can mitigate dependence on any singular major power, offering alternative markets and bolstered resilience for ASEAN's goods and services.

Secondly, ASEAN's robust foundation positions it well to foster regional, technologically enabled economic integration and cooperation. Collaborative endeavours can amplify the collective bargaining power of ASEAN countries, culminating in a more robust technopolitical and economic ecosystem amidst global uncertainties. Prioritising the development of a robust digital economy and supporting innovative start-ups allow the region to capitalise on emerging technologies and usher in new economic prospects.

Thirdly, given the dynamic nature of global politics and technology, ASEAN's continuous vigilance over geopolitical and technopolitical developments, both within and beyond the purview of the United States and China, is paramount. A well-informed and prepared stance is indispensable to enable the region to respond effectively to fluctuations and transformations, concurrently fostering a stabilising force on the global technological and economic stage.

Fourthly, acknowledging the potential risks of restricted access to critical technologies due to the US–China competition, ASEAN countries should consider collaborative investments in research, development, and innovation. While each nation has its unique economic, social, and intellectual foundation, collective efforts to nurture indigenous technological capabilities may yield substantial benefits. While an independent ASEAN technological ecosystem may be unwarranted and counterproductive, prioritising home-grown innovation is pivotal to decreasing reliance on external technology providers.

To thrive within the forthcoming technological landscape, ASEAN countries must address vulnerabilities in planning and adopting advanced technologies on their own terms. For instance, in the realm of data protection, reliance on advanced technologies from both the United States and China may entail drawbacks. However, the lack of robust regulations could lead to similar data misuse issues, even in the absence of foreign entities.[13]

Moreover, to attract technology investments and foster collaboration, ASEAN should strategically position itself as an alluring destination for new research and development centres. By offering an enabling business environment, robust intellectual property safeguards, and a skilled workforce — particularly in more developed member states like Singapore — ASEAN can entice companies from both the United States and China to expand their presence in the region. Concurrently, adapting and revising trade and investment policies can render ASEAN more responsive to emerging economic trends and geopolitical shifts, thereby sustaining its attractiveness as a hub.

Lastly, ASEAN, as a coordinating entity, should steadfastly uphold neutrality and pragmatism in the realm of technopolitics. This role is pivotal in continuing to serve the region's interests. Serving as a bridge between and beyond the two superpowers, ASEAN holds the potential to facilitate dialogue, negotiation, and cooperation, ultimately

---

[13] Jun-E. Tan, "What does the US-China AI Rivalry mean for Southeast Asia?", *The Diplomat*, 7 February 2022, https://thediplomat.com/2022/02/what-does-the-us-china-ai-rivalry-mean-for-southeast-asia/.

contributing to the greater good of the international community in the realm of technological evolution and development.

Conclusion

In a world where advanced technology sectors hold paramount importance for global economies, third-party nations, particularly entities like the ASEAN member states, are tasked with the intricate challenge of meticulously weighing their interests and strategically adapting to the fluid dynamics of technological relations. Furthermore, achieving a delicate equilibrium between concerns pertaining to national security and the practicalities of economic realities stands as a pivotal endeavour, one that safeguards the advantages of both global and regional development, thereby ensuring the enduring protection of national interests.

Undoubtedly, the United States will persist in curbing China's access to technology, products, and future opportunities, while China's responsive measures, which might include assertive reactions, can be predicted to a certain extent. In this context, it becomes arduous, if not implausible, for ASEAN and other third-party entities to entirely evade the repercussions of the US–China competition. Nevertheless, amidst this complex milieu, the imperative of multilateral cooperation and responsible governance looms even larger, constituting pivotal pillars for the preservation of global stability and security.

ASEAN is well poised to adopt a proactive and well-balanced approach to address the challenges posed by the US–China technological rivalry. While ASEAN countries and their leaders stand firm against a binary zero-sum mentality and resist aligning with either side, it is imperative to acknowledge that such a stance may attract criticism and counterforces from factions driven by more polarised perspectives, interests, and predilections. It is, in essence, a test of rational discernment, steadfast resolve, and astute statecraft. By diversifying their trade partners, fostering an environment of innovation, forging robust partnerships, and steadfastly upholding neutrality and pragmatism, ASEAN countries can effectively mitigate potential risks and harness newfound opportunities within the ever-evolving global technological landscape.

CHAPTER 3

US–China Technology Competition: US Aims and Interests

Adrian Ang

Introduction

The strategic competition between the United States and the People's Republic of China to be the world's dominant superpower takes on multiple dimensions: from trade to human rights, ideology and competing visions of global governance, and the ordering of the international system. However, a high-stakes competition over advanced technologies lies at the heart of the increasingly acrimonious strategic rivalry between Washington and Beijing. For the United States, the technology competition with China encompasses areas of economics, national security, and geopolitics. Under the Trump and Biden administrations, the United States has adopted steps to deny China access to certain critical and sensitive dual-use technologies, particularly in the areas of artificial intelligence (AI), advanced semiconductors, 5G, and other emerging areas of the so-called Fourth Industrial Revolution.

US National Security Concerns Over Chinese Tech — The Blurring of the Public and Private

The lines between the public and private spheres have become increasingly fuzzy as the Chinese Communist Party (CCP) attempts to assert greater control over Chinese society.[1] US officials are particularly concerned about the vagueness of the Chinese regulatory and legal framework pertaining to technology and national security. China's National Security Law instructs all citizens to support, assist, and cooperate with intelligence work.[2] The Cybersecurity Law requires Chinese companies to store data within the country and network operators to "provide technical support and assistance" to state security agencies.[3] The 2017 National Intelligence Law enjoins all Chinese organisations and citizens to support, assist, and cooperate with national intelligence operations.[4] Further, by law, Chinese technology companies — like all companies in the country — have embedded CCP cells. Jack Ma, the co-founder of Alibaba, was revealed to be a party member,[5] while Huawei's founder Ren Zhengfei is also a party member

[1] Simon Denyer, "Xi Jinping at China congress calls on party to tighten its grip on the country", *Washington Post*, 18 October 2017, www.washingtonpost.com/world/asia_pacific/confidence-control-paranoia-mark-xi-jinpings-speech-at-china-party-congress/2017/10/18/6e618694-b373-11e7-9b93-b97043e57a22_story.html.

[2] Covington, *China Enacts National Security Law*, (Washington, D.C.: Covington & Burling LLP, 2015), pp. 1–3, www.cov.com/~/media/files/corporate/publications/2015/06/china_passes_new_national_security_law.pdf.

[3] Ashley Feng, "We can't tell if Chinese firms work for the party", *Foreign Policy*, 7 February 2019, https://foreignpolicy.com/2019/02/07/we-cant-tell-if-chinese-firms-work-for-the-party/.

[4] Chinese National People's Congress Network, "National intelligence law of the People's Republic", 27 June 2017, https://cs.brown.edu/courses/csci1800/sources/2017_PRC_NationalIntelligenceLaw.pdf.

[5] *Reuters*, "Alibaba's Jack Ma is a communist party member, China state paper reveals", *Reuters*, 27 November 2018, www.reuters.com/article/us-alibaba-jack-ma/alibabas-jack-ma-is-a-communist-party-member-china-state-paper-reveals-idUSKCN1NW073.

and the former director of the Information Engineering Academy of the People Liberation Army (PLA).[6]

US officials are especially concerned by the blurring of lines between the Chinese party-state and the private sphere occurring under the concept of Military–Civil Fusion (MCF), which seeks to break down barriers to create stronger linkages between China's civilian economy and the defence industrial base. This would "create and leverage synergies between economic development and military modernization, allowing the defense and commercial enterprises to collaborate and synchronize their efforts through the sharing of talent, resources, and innovations".[7] There is disagreement, however, among scholars about how much scrutiny should be placed on MCF: some argue that MCF is more myth than reality; others point to the PLA successfully exploiting commercial developments for its modernisation drive; and still others argue that China's current capabilities and the rationale behind MCF are of great importance.[8]

Nonetheless, US officials have taken to interpreting China's vague national security laws, the apparent cosy relationship between Chinese technology companies and the CCP, and the MCF concept to mean that Chinese technology companies pose a national security threat as they are subject to direct orders from the Chinese party-state. Indeed, MCF

---

6   Chua Kong Ho, "Huawei founder Ren Zhengfei on why he joined China's communist party and the People's Liberation Army", *South China Morning Post*, 16 January 2019, www.scmp.com/tech/big-tech/article/2182332/huawei-founder-ren-zhengfei-why-he-joined-chinas-communist-party-and.

7   Elsa B. Kania and Lorand Laskai, *Myths and Realities of China's Military-Civil Fusion Strategy*, CNAS Technology & National Security Report, (Washington, D.C.: Center for a New American Security, 2021), 1–23, www.cnas.org/publications/reports/myths-and-realities-of-chinas-military-civil-fusion-strategy.

8   *Ibid.*; Richard A. Bitzinger, "China's shift from civil-military integration to military-civil fusion", *Asia Policy* 16 no. 1 (2021): 20–23; Emily Weinstein, "Don't Underestimate China's Military-Civil Fusion Efforts", *Foreign Policy*, 5 February 2021, https://foreignpolicy.com/2021/02/05/dont-underestimate-chinas-military-civil-fusion-efforts/.

has been deemed the "key analytic driver" in the intensifying economic and technological competition between Beijing and Washington.[9]

The National Security Imperative and Technology Policy

After President Donald Trump declared a "national emergency" over threats to the US communications networks posed by "foreign adversaries" in May 2019,[10] the US government proceeded to purge Chinese telecoms companies and their equipment and services from American networks on national security grounds.[11] The Trump administration also moved to ban TikTok and WeChat from the US market on national security grounds. In August 2020, President Trump issued executive orders to prohibit Americans from carrying out any transactions with the Chinese parent companies of TikTok and WeChat — ByteDance and Tencent, respectively.[12] A federal judge, however, blocked the administration's move to ban WeChat and the Biden administration rescinded Trump's executive order, arguing that further evaluation was required.[13]

[9] Elsa B. Kania and Lorand Laskai, (2021), *Op. cit.*

[10] Samuel Bendett and Elsa B. Kania, "Chinese and Russian defense innovation, with American characteristics? — Military innovation, commercial technologies, and great power competition", *The Strategy Bridge*, 2 August 2018, https://thestrategybridge.org/the-bridge/2018/8/2/chinese-and-russian-defense-innovation-with-american-characteristics-military-innovation-commercial-technologies-and-great-power-competition.

[11] Christian Vasquez and Elias Groll, "FCC faces long road in stripping Chinese tech from US telecom networks", *Cyberscoop*, 30 November 2022, https://cyberscoop.com/fcc-huawei-zte-security-risks/.

[12] "Executive order on addressing the threat posed by TikTok", *Trump White House Archives*, 6 August 2020, https://trumpwhitehouse.archives.gov/presidential-actions/executive-order-addressing-threat-posed-tiktok/.

[13] Bobby Allyn, "Federal judge blocks trump administration's US WeChat Ban", *National Public Radio*, 20 September 2020, www.npr.org/2020/09/20/914983610/federal-judge-blocks-trump-administrations-u-s-wechat-ban; Bobby Allyn, "Biden drops Trump's Ban on TikTok and WeChat — But will continue the scrutiny", *National Public Radio*, 9 June 2021, www.npr.org/2021/06/09/1004750274/biden-replaces-trump-bans-on-tiktok-wechat-with-order-to-scrutinize-apps.

The Biden administration has revived efforts to ban TikTok, with strong bipartisan support in Congress. In March 2023, TikTok's CEO Shou Zi Chew testified before the US Congress and faced intense grilling from lawmakers who accused the company of serving as a Trojan Horse for Chinese influence, disinformation, and collecting reams of sensitive data on US users.[14] Shou strenuously denied that the app shares data or has connections with the Chinese Communist Party. Zhou stated that the company had spent more than two years on "Project Texas" to seal off protected US user data from unauthorised foreign access[15] and that "American data is stored on American soil, by an American company, overseen by American personnel".[16] Lawmakers were unconvinced and TikTok has been banned on US federal government devices,[17] was pressured to divest by the Committee on Foreign Investment in the United States (CFIUS) or face a ban,[18] and was subject to a complete state ban in Montana.[19]

14   Jenn Brice, "TikTok is collecting an 'excessive' amount of data from users, report suggests", *Marketing Brew*, 2 August 2022, www.marketingbrew.com/stories/2022/08/02/tiktok-is-collecting-an-excessive-amount-of-data-from-users-report-suggests.

15   Emily Baker-White, "Inside project Texas, TikTok's big answer to US Lawmakers' China fears", *BuzzFeed News*, 11 March 2022, www.buzzfeednews.com/article/emilybakerwhite/tiktok-project-texas-bytedance-user-data.

16   David Shepardson and Rami Ayyub, "TikTok congressional hearing: CEO Shou Zi Chew grilled by US lawmakers", *Reuters*, 24 March 2023, www.reuters.com/technology/tiktok-ceo-face-tough-questions-support-us-ban-grows-2023-03-23/.

17   Kari Paul, "US bans China-based TikTok app on all federal government devices", *The Guardian*, 30 December 2022, www.theguardian.com/technology/2022/dec/30/us-tiktok-ban-government-devices-china.

18   Yifan Lu and Cissy Zhou, "U.S. orders ByteDance to divest TikTok or face potential ban", *Nikkei Asia*, 16 March 2023, https://asia.nikkei.com/Business/Technology/U.S.-orders-ByteDance-to-divest-TikTok-or-face-potential-ban.

19   Amy Beth Hanson and Haleluya Hadero, "Montana says 1st-in-nation TikTok ban protects people. TikTok says it violates their rights", *The Associated Press*, 19 May 2023, https://apnews.com/article/tiktok-ban-montana-325a33578a2bbfbe53e9c251d528c5fb.

US Export Controls and Semiconductors

When President Trump signed the executive order barring US companies from doing business with Huawei in May 2019, the US Commerce Department placed Huawei on its "Entity List", which restricted it from buying US products without an export licence.[20] At the time, Huawei was the global market leader in wireless 5G infrastructure and the world's largest manufacturer of mobile phones. The sanctions have proved tremendously costly. Huawei saw its share of the mobile phone market plummet, and its chip design arm, HiSilicon, saw its share in the global smartphone chipset market reduced to zero, resulting in a collapse in revenue.[21] Furthermore, its attempted reinvention as a cloud service and business solutions provider is now under threat from a total US export ban.[22]

The Trump administration's export controls against Huawei revealed China's dependence on companies located in the US and allied countries for the supply of advanced semiconductors. However, manufacturing advanced chips is an extremely complex process, and there are only a handful of companies able to operate at the cutting edge of the

[20] David Shepardson and Karen Freifeld, "China's Huawei, 70 affiliates placed on U.S. trade blacklist", *Reuters*, 16 May 2019, www.reuters.com/article/us-usa-china-huaweitech-idUSKCN1SL2W4.

[21] Dashveenjit Kaur, "Huawei has ran out of chips for smartphones as US sanction crippled the Chinese telecom giant", *Techwire Asia*, 23 December 2022, https://techwireasia.com/2022/12/huawei-has-ran-out-of-chips-for-smartphones-as-us-sanction-crippled-the-chinese-telecom-giant/; Ewdison Then, "Huawei is no longer in the top 5 of the smartphone market", *Slash Gear*, 20 April 2021, https://www.slashgear.com/huawei-is-no-longer-in-the-top-5-of-the-smartphone-market-21669716.

[22] Dashveenjit Kaur, "The US is not done attacking Huawei — A complete ban is looming around the corner", *Techwire Asia*, 1 February 2023, https://techwireasia.com/2023/02/the-us-is-not-done-hobbling-huawei-a-complete-ban-is-looming-around-the-corner/; Takashi Kawakami, Risa Kawaba, and Rintaro Tobita, "Huawei's rebirth as cloud provider faces total US export ban threat", *Nikkei Asia*, 3 March 2023, https://asia.nikkei.com/Spotlight/Huawei-crackdown/Huawei-s-rebirth-as-cloud-provider-faces-total-U.S.-export-ban-threat.

semiconductor industry. Crucially, none of them are in China.[23] This dependence on the West renders China highly vulnerable to being cut off from the supply of advanced semiconductors and being prevented from indigenising advanced chipmaking capabilities, thereby sustaining China's dependence on and vulnerability to the democracies.[24] The United States and its democratic allies — especially Japan, South Korea, the Netherlands, and Taiwan — command critical "chokepoints" in the global semiconductor value chain, thereby allowing the United States to throttle China's chips industry and limit its access to, and development of, advanced technologies.[25] Hence, the Biden administration's sweeping export controls on 7 October 2022 targeted three critical chokepoints: AI chips, Electronic Design Automation (EDA) tools, and photolithography equipment.

The Biden Administration's 7 October 2022 Export Controls
Banning the Export of AI Chips

The PLA has sought to adopt AI as part of its "intelligentization" of warfare to increase the tempo of military operations.[26] However, the PLA's progress in this field requires continued access to advanced AI chips whose market leaders are US firms Nvidia, Advanced Micro

---

[23] See Chris Miller, *Chip Wars: The Fight for the World's Most Critical Technology,* (New York: Scribner, 2022).

[24] See Saif M. Khan, *Securing Semiconductor Supply Chains*, CSET Analysis (Washington, D.C.: Center for Security and Emergency Technology, 2021), pp. 1–71, doi:10.51593/20190017.

[25] See Andre Barbe and Will Hunt, *Preserving the Chokepoints: Reducing the Risk of Offshoring Among US Semiconductor Manufacturing Equipment Firms*, CSET Analysis (Washington, D.C.: Center for Security and Emergency Technology, 2022), pp. 1–20, doi:10.51593/20210045.

[26] See Elsa B. Kania, "Artificial intelligence in future Chinese command decision making", in *Artificial Intelligence, China, Russia, and the Global Order*, ed. Nicholas C. Wright, (Alabama: Air University Press, 2019), pp. 153–161.

Devices (AMD), and Intel. Both the Trump and Biden administrations have attempted to limit the PLA's access to these chips based on end-user export controls, but US regulators have found it difficult to wage a targeted crackdown on the PLA's intermediary chip suppliers.[27] The Biden administration's solution to the military end-user conundrum was to abandon end-user controls entirely in favour of a blanket export ban of advanced AI chips to China.[28] Further, the United States invoked the foreign direct product rule in the export ban on AI chips, ensuring that the restrictions extend not only to US chips but also to those from any would-be foreign competitor.

Export controls on semiconductor manufacturing equipment

The 7 October export controls also targeted advanced semiconductor manufacturing equipment (SME) to prevent China from developing domestic alternatives to Nvidia and AMD AI chips. The export controls targeted EDA tools needed to design, validate, and monitor the chip manufacturing process and the equipment to fabricate them.[29] China's domestic chip industry is extremely dependent on foreign EDA software. Chinese chip companies that have made breakthroughs at the 5–7-nm threshold have all relied on foreign EDA tools. The 7 October export

---

[27] See Ryan Fedasiuk, Karson Elmgren, and Ellen Lu, *Silicon Twist: Managing the Chinese Military's Access to AI Chips*, CSET Analysis (Washington, D.C.: Center for Security and Emergency Technology, 2022), pp. 1–36, doi:10.51593/20210068.

[28] Gregory C. Allen, *Choking off China's Access to the Future of AI*, CSIS Analysis (Washington, D.C.: Center for Strategic and International Studies, 2022), pp. 1–10, www.csis.org/analysis/choking-chinas-access-future-ai; Stephen Nellis and Jane Lee, "U.S. officials order Nvidia to halt sales of top AI chips to China", *Reuters*, 1 September 2022, www.reuters.com/technology/nvidia-says-us-has-imposed-new-license-requirement-future-exports-china-2022-08-31/.

[29] Bureau of Industry and Security, "Commerce Implements New Multilateral Controls on Advanced Semiconductor and Gas Turbine Engine Technologies", 12 August 2022, www.bis.doc.gov/index.php/documents/about-bis/newsroom/press-releases/3116-2022-08-12-bis-press-release-wa-2021-1758-technologies-controls-rule/file.

control rules also blocked US chip equipment makers Applied Materials, Lam Research, and KLA from shipping tools for advanced chipmaking to Chinese clients, and restricted US nationals from working with Chinese chipmakers.[30] The 7 October export controls on SME also targeted photolithography equipment needed to print the miniscule transistors on the surface of silicon wafers. However, unlike AI chips and EDA tools where US firms are dominant, photolithography is dominated by companies from the Netherlands and Japan, such as ASML, Tokyo Electron Limited, Nikon, and Canon.

For the US export controls on SME to effectively deny China the ability to manufacture its own advanced chips, the Japanese and Dutch governments would also have to impose similar export bans on their key suppliers. In January 2023, Biden met with both Japanese Prime Minister Fumio Kishida and Dutch Prime Minister Mark Rutte in Washington to secure their support for the US export controls.[31] In March 2023, the Dutch government said it would issue new restrictions on exports of semiconductor technology to protect national security but did not mention China by name.[32] In June, ASML announced that export control rules would affect sales of its advanced immersive deep ultraviolet (DUV) lithography systems to China.[33] Similarly,

---

[30] Allen, (2022), *Op. cit.*

[31] See *Al Jazeera*, "Biden, Dutch PM Rutte discuss China, Ukraine at White House meet", *Al Jazeera*, 17 January 2023. www.aljazeera.com/news/2023/1/17/china-tech-access-expected-to-top-biden-dutch-pm-rutte-meeting; David Brunnstrom and Michael Martina, "Biden, Kishida held 'very productive' talks on China export controls", *Reuters*, 18 January 2023, www.reuters.com/world/biden-raised-issue-export-controls-china-with-japans-kishida-us-official-2023-01-17/.

[32] Toby Sterling, Karen Freifield, and Alexandra Alper, "Dutch to restrict semiconductor tech exports to China, joining US effort", *Reuters*, 9 March 2023, www.reuters.com/technology/dutch-responds-us-china-policy-with-plan-curb-semiconductor-tech-exports-2023-03-08/.

[33] Cheng Ting-fang, Lauly Li, and Rhyannon Imadegawa-Bartlett, "Netherlands unveils chip tool export curbs in fresh blow to China", *Nikkei Asia*, 30 June 2023, https://asia.nikkei.com/Business/Tech/Semiconductors/Netherlands-unveils-chip-tool-export-curbs-in-fresh-blow-to-China.

in May 2023, the Japanese government announced that it was adding 23 items to its list of regulated exports, including advanced SME for extreme ultraviolet lithography and etching equipment for stacking memory devices in three dimensions.[34] Japan's export controls would go into effect in July 2023 and did not specify China by name.

The Biden Administration's Executive Order on US Investments in Chinese Tech

On 9 August 2023, President Biden signed a long-anticipated executive order to enact outbound US investment restrictions in three sensitive technology sectors in China: semiconductors, quantum information technologies, and artificial intelligence.[35] The Treasury Department concurrently issued an advance notice of proposed rulemaking (ANPRM) seeking to prohibit some new US investment in China in those sensitive technologies and to require government notification in other sectors.[36]

The Treasury Department's proposed prohibitions on investment in semiconductors in China covers much the same ground as the 7 October export controls, as it seeks to close loopholes to prevent companies from assisting China in developing the sanctioned

---

[34] *Nikkei Asia*, "Japan chip export curb to China will take effect in July", *Nikkei Asia*, 23 May 2023, https://asia.nikkei.com/Business/Tech/Semiconductors/Japan-chip-export-curb-to-China-will-take-effect-in-July.

[35] The White House, "Executive order on addressing United States investments in certain national security technologies and products in countries of concern", 9 August 2023, www.whitehouse.gov/briefing-room/presidential-actions/2023/08/09/executive-order-on-addressing-united-states-investments-in-certain-national-security-technologies-and-products-in-countries-of-concern/.

[36] Office of Investment Security, Department of the Treasury, provisions pertaining to U.S. investments in certain national security, 14 August 2023, https://public-inspection.federalregister.gov/2023-17164.pdf.

technologies through investments and know-how.[37] The Treasury is seeking to prohibit investments that assist China in designing and producing advanced semiconductors; in fabricating and packaging advanced chips; and in installing supercomputers powered by advanced chips.[38] However, unlike the 7 October export controls, the Treasury's proposed restrictions on investments in quantum computing and AI systems are limited to targeting military, intelligence, and security end uses, rather than the entire Chinese economy.[39]

The Treasury Department has also proposed notification requirements for some types of investment in semiconductors and AI systems in China. This proposed notification regime has been often described as a "reverse Committee on Foreign Investment in the United States (CFIUS)"[40] — a reference to the Committee on Foreign Investment in the United States, which reviews foreign investment in the US. However, the Treasury's advanced notice suggests that, unlike CFIUS, it will not review transactions on a case-by-case basis, thereby reducing the risk of an overburdened regulatory process.[41] The Treasury is proposing

---

[37] The White House, "Background press call by senior administration officials previewing executive order on addressing U.S. Investments in certain national security technologies and products in countries of concern", 10 August 2023, www.whitehouse.gov/briefing-room/press-briefings/2023/08/10/background-press-call-by-senior-administration-officials-previewing-executive-order-on-addressing-u-s-investments-in-certain-national-security-technologies-and-products-in-countries-of-concern/; Emily Benson and Gregory C. Allen, *A New National Security Instrument: The Executive Order on Outbound Investment*, CSIS Commentary (Washington, D.C.: Center for Strategic and International Studies, 2023), www.csis.org/analysis/new-national-security-instrument-executive-order-outbound-investment.

[38] Office of Investment Security, Department of the treasury, *Provisions*, p. 101.

[39] *Ibid.*, pp. 128, 145.

[40] Jack Stone Truitt, "Biden executive order on investments in China faces hurdles", *Nikkei Asia*, 10 June 2023, https://asia.nikkei.com/Politics/International-relations/US-China-tensions/Biden-executive-order-on-investments-in-China-faces-hurdles.

[41] Office of Investment Security, *Op. cit.*, p. 20.

notifications to be filed within 30 days for investments in the designing, fabricating, and packaging of legacy chips in China and investments in AI systems that are primarily designed for cybersecurity, facial recognition, robotics, and intelligence gathering.[42]

The Impact of Export Controls and Investment Restrictions

Singapore's Foreign Minister Vivian Balakrishnan has described the 7 October export controls as "all but a declaration of a technology war".[43] They are a sharp departure from the traditional US export control policy of denying China state-of-the-art technology but allowing the export of older technology, which would be modified accordingly as new technologies are developed and emerged.[44] This "sliding scale" policy had the advantage of maintaining America's relative lead by denying China access to the most advanced technology while still allowing US firms to sell older technologies and reducing incentives for China to develop domestic alternatives. However, in a September 2022 speech, US National Security Adviser Jake Sullivan argued that the old "sliding scale" policy of staying a couple of generations ahead of China was no longer feasible given the "foundational nature of certain technologies, such as advanced logic and memory chips" and that the US must now

---

[42] Ibid., *Provisions*, p. 177.

[43] Singapore Ministry of Foreign Affairs, "Transcript of minister for foreign affairs Dr Vivian Balakrishnan's remarks at the second Next Step Global Conference 2022 at Raffles Hotel on 9 November 2022", 10 November 2022, www.mfa.gov.sg/Newsroom/Press-Statements-Transcripts-and-Photos/2022/11/221110nextstep.

[44] See William Reinsch and Emily Benson, "Chipping away at global semiconductor supply chains", *Hinrich Foundation*, 11 July 2023, www.hinrichfoundation.com/research/article/tech/chipping-away-at-global-semiconductor-supply-chains/.

"maintain as large of a lead as possible".[45] To maintain an absolute advantage over China, the US weaponised its — and its allies' — chokeholds in the global semiconductor value chain to not merely deny China access to advanced chips but to also prevent it from acquiring the wherewithal to manufacture them.

With the 7 October export controls, the Biden administration also signalled that the United States was no longer content with merely targeting individual Chinese companies like Huawei — it was targeting China's entire semiconductor industry and technology ecosystem. By permanently maintaining export controls at a fixed level regardless of future technological developments, China's entire technology ecosystem will degrade over time while the rest of the world advances. So, although the export controls are ostensibly aimed at stifling the PLA and the Chinese security state apparatus, their externalities will affect the whole of Chinese society.

China has denounced the 7 October export controls as the "weaponization and politicization" of science and technology, a US attempt to maintain its "sci-tech hegemony", and the malicious blocking and suppressing of Chinese companies.[46] Beijing initiated a dispute against the US at the World Trade Organization (WTO), accusing it of abusing export control measures and obstructing normal international trade in chips.[47] China also banned the use of US-based Micron

---

[45] The White House, "Remarks by national security advisor Jake Sullivan at the special competitive studies project global emerging technologies summit", 16 September 2022, www.whitehouse.gov/briefing-room/speeches-remarks/2022/09/16/remarks-by-national-security-advisor-jake-sullivan-at-the-special-competitive-studies-project-global-emerging-technologies-summit/.

[46] *The Associated Press*, "China lashes out at latest U.S. export controls on chips", *The Associated Press*, 8 October 2022, https://apnews.com/article/technology-business-china-global-trade-47eed4a9fa1c2f51027ed12cf929ff55.

[47] Arjun Kharpal, "China brings WTO case against U.S. and its sweeping chip export curbs as tech tensions escalate", *CNBC*, 13 December 2022, www.cnbc.com/2022/12/13/china-brings-wto-case-against-us-chip-export-restrictions.html.

Technology's chips in certain sectors.[48] In July 2023, China announced that it was placing export restrictions on gallium and germanium, two metals widely used in semiconductors.[49] China's relatively muted response to the 7 October export controls attests to the fact that Beijing lacks any significant leverage against Washington and its allies and fears even harsher reprisal measures.

In the short term, China has no domestic alternatives to advanced US AI chips. To meet the nigh-insatiable demand from the Chinese market and to combat the lucrative black market for the embargoed chips,[50] Nvidia has designed downgraded export-control-compliant versions of its two most advanced chips to service the China market — the A800 and H800.[51] However, these downgraded chips

[48]   *Reuters*, "China fails Micron's products in security review, bars some purchases", *Reuters*, 22 May 2023, www.reuters.com/technology/chinas-regulator-says-finds-serious-security-issues-us-micron-technologys-2023-05-21/.

[49]   Amy Lv and Brenda Goh, "Beijing jabs in US-China tech fight with chip material export curbs", *Reuters*, 5 July 2023, www.reuters.com/technology/us-firm-axt-applying-permits-after-china-restricts-chipmaking-exports-2023-07-04/.

[50]   See *Reuters*, "Focus: Inside China's underground market for high-end Nvidia AI chips", *Reuters*, 21 June 2023, www.reuters.com/technology/inside-chinas-underground-market-high-end-nvidia-ai-chips-2023-06-19/; Che Pan and Iris Deng, "Tech war: Strong demand in China for advanced chips used on AI projects creates growing market for smuggled Nvidia GPUs, despite US ban", *South China Morning Post*, 27 June 2023, www.scmp.com/tech/tech-war/article/3225594/tech-war-strong-demand-china-advanced-chips-used-ai-projects-creates-growing-market-smuggled-nvidia?module=inline&pgtype=article.

[51]   Stephen Nellis and Jane Lee, "Nvidia tweaks flagship H100 chip for export to China as H800", *Reuters*, 22 March 2023, www.reuters.com/technology/nvidia-tweaks-flagship-h100-chip-export-china-h800-2023-03-21/; Jane Lee, "Exclusive: Nvidia offers new advanced chip for China that meets U.S. export controls", *Reuters*, 8 November 2022, www.reuters.com/technology/exclusive-nvidia-offers-new-advanced-chip-china-that-meets-us-export-controls-2022-11-08/. Intel has followed Nvidia's lead and produced a modified version of its GPU for the Chinese market. AMD is also considering making a specific export control-compliant AI chip for China. See Dashveenjit Kaur, "Intel joins Nvidia in tackling the US ban with an AI chip for China", *Techwire Asia*, 14 July 2023, https://techwireasia.com/2023/07/intel-joins-nvidia-in-tackling-the-us-ban-with-an-ai-chip-for-china/; Arjun Kharpal, "AMD considers making a specific A.I. chip for China to comply with export controls", *CNBC*, 2 August 2023, www.cnbc.com/2023/08/02/amd-considers-specific-china-ai-chip-to-comply-with-us-export-curbs.html.

are merely a stopgap measure since US export controls can be tweaked in the future to target even these lower-performance AI chips.[52] China also stockpiled advanced DUV machines to enable the manufacturing of 7-nm chips,[53] but the new Japanese and Dutch export control regulations will affect Nikon or ASML's ability to provide maintenance, repairs, or spare parts to controlled equipment in China.[54] Thus, even if Chinese companies are able to produce relatively advanced 7-nm chips, their ability to do so over time will be compromised and degraded given the dearth of domestic alternatives to repair or replace critical lithographic equipment.

The 9 August investment restrictions are not expected to be as immediately impactful as the 7 October export controls. The investment restrictions were designed to complement the 7 October export controls rather than to disrupt China's economy or decouple the two countries' highly interdependent economies.[55] The investment restrictions are expected to affect relatively few transactions as they come in the midst of declining US tech investments in China due to the COVID-19 pandemic and the geopolitical tensions between Washington and

---

[52] Fearing additional US sanctions, China's tech giants rushed to stockpile Nvidia's chips, with the *Financial Times* reporting that Tencent, Alibaba, and Baidu have made orders worth US$1 billion to acquire about 100,000 A800 chips to be delivered in 2023 and a further US$4 billion worth of GPUs to be delivered in 2024. See *Financial Times*, "China's internet giants order $5bn of Nvidia chips to power AI ambitions", *Financial Times*, 9 August 2023, www.ft.com/content/9dfee156-4870-4ca4-b67d-bb5a285d855c.

[53] Mathieu Duchâtel, "Great power chokepoints: China's semiconductor industry in search of breakthroughs", in *Expressions by Montaigne* (Paris, France: Institute Montaigne, 2022), p. 6, www.institutmontaigne.org/ressources/pdfs/publications/great-power-chokepoints-chinas-semiconductor-industry-search-breakthroughs.pdf.

[54] Cagan Koc, Jillian Deutsch, and Alberto Nardelli, "ASML faces tighter Dutch restrictions on servicing chip equipment in China", *Bloomberg*, 15 July 2023, www.bloomberg.com/news/articles/2023-07-14/asml-faces-tighter-restrictions-on-servicing-chip-gear-in-china#xj4y7vzkg.

[55] The White House, *Background Press Call Previewing Executive Order on Addressing U.S. Investments*.

Beijing.[56] Another limitation of the investment restrictions is the extent to which the US can convince or compel its allies to adopt similar measures. As with the 7 October export controls, the investment restrictions need to be multilateralised or they can simply be circumvented. The EU is set to establish its own outbound investment screening initiative by the end of the year, but it remains unclear if Europe will adopt the Biden administration's restrictions wholesale.[57]

That is not to say, however, that the investment restrictions lack the potential for expansion and escalation. The Treasury Department's advance notice includes requests for comment on additional technologies where investments should be restricted and proposes an annual review process to modify the investment controls.[58] Also, although existing export controls omit quantum computing and AI systems, the door remains open to their future inclusion, and to the inclusion of biotechnology and renewable energy, which the Biden administration has identified as "foundational technologies" in which the United States must maintain as large a lead over China as possible.[59]

---

[56] Kevin Klyman, "Biden takes measured approach on China investment controls", *Foreign Policy*, 19 August 2023, https://foreignpolicy.com/2023/08/19/biden-approach-china-economy-investment-control/.

[57] Finbarr Bermingham, "Biden plan to curb China investments focuses EU minds as deadline looms", *South China Morning Post*, 19 August 2023, www.scmp.com/news/china/diplomacy/article/3231506/biden-plan-curb-china-investments-focuses-eu-minds-deadline-looms.

[58] Office of Investment Security, *Op. cit.*, p. 24.

[59] See for example, The White House, (2022), *Op. cit.*; The White House, "Remarks by national security advisor Jake Sullivan on renewing American Economic Leadership at the Brookings Institution", 27 April 2023, www.whitehouse.gov/briefing-room/speeches-remarks/2023/04/27/remarks-by-national-security-advisor-jake-sullivan-on-renewing-american-economic-leadership-at-the-brookings-institution/; U.S. Department of Commerce, "Remarks by U.S. secretary of commerce Gina Raimondo on the U.S. competitiveness and the China challenge", 30 November 2022, www.commerce.gov/news/speeches/2022/11/remarks-us-secretary-commerce-gina-raimondo-us-competitiveness-and-china; Alan F. Estevez, *A Conversation with Under Secretary of*

Conclusion

The US export controls and investment restrictions on China's technology sector create formidable obstacles to China's indigenisation of a supply chain capable of producing embargoed advanced computer chips. This will not stop China from trying, however; if access to these advanced chips were considered a national security priority previously, they have now taken on an existential importance. China has already attempted to evade the controls through smuggling and renting access to American cloud computing services and quietly reviving its controversial Thousand Talents Plan (TTP) under a new name to poach foreign technology talent.[60]

Over the longer term, the technology restrictions could pose serious challenges for US companies seeking to maintain their market share and preserve their technological advantages. China is the most important global market for semiconductor exports, accounting for one-third of sales in the US$574 billion market in 2022.[61] It is simply unrealistic to expect firms — US or otherwise — to abandon that market. Further, as technology advances and the US restrictions expand to cover more equipment and services, it will incentivise innovations to eliminate US-sourced technologies to avoid America's broad extraterritorial restrictions and sanctions.

Commerce Alan F. Estevez, by Martijin Rasser, CNAS Transcript, (Washington, D.C.: Center for a New American Security, 2022), www.cnas.org/publications/transcript/a-conversation-with-under-secretary-of-commerce-alan-f-estevez.

[60] See Tim Fist, Lennart Heim, and Jordan Schneider, "Chinese firms are evading chip controls", *Foreign Policy,* 21 June 2023, https://foreignpolicy.com/2023/06/21/china-united-states-semiconductor-chips-sanctions-evasion/; Julie Zhu *et al.* "Insight: China quietly recruits overseas chip talent as US tightens curbs", *Reuters,* 25 August 2023, www.reuters.com/technology/china-quietly-recruits-overseas-chip-talent-us-tightens-curbs-2023-08-24/.

[61] See Semiconductor Industry Association, "Global semiconductor sales increase 3.3% in 2022 despite second-half slowdown", 3 February 2023, www.semiconductors.org/global-semiconductor-sales-increase-3-2-in-2022-despite-second-half-slowdown/.

Here, Huawei's experience of US export controls might prove instructive. Cut off from US chips and the tools to design its own chips, Huawei saw revenues plummet but ploughed huge sums into R&D, replaced over 13,000 parts in its products that were subject to US sanctions with domestic Chinese substitutes, and redesigned 4,000 circuit boards for its products.[62] Despite US export controls and sanctions, Huawei remains a global leader in 5G technology and is poised to return to the smartphone market.[63] Thus, Nvidia — even amidst reporting record profits[64] — has warned that additional export curbs on advanced chips would risk a "permanent loss" for American semiconductor firms in one of the world's largest markets.[65] Previously, casualties of the US–China technology competition have primarily fallen on the Chinese side — like Huawei and ZTE — but now US SME companies like Applied Materials and Lam Research are seeing the competition take a toll on their revenues.[66]

US technology restrictions on China present opportunities for some countries in Southeast Asia, as US firms shift their supply chains out

---

[62]   Stephen Nellis and Krystal Hu, "Huawei has replaced thousands of U.S.-banned parts in its products, founder says", *Reuters*, 18 March 2023, www.reuters.com/technology/huawei-has-replaced-thousands-us-banned-parts-its-products-founder-says-2023-03-18/.

[63]   Yifan Yu and Cheng Ting-Fang, "Huawei returns to global stage with focus on 5G and the cloud", *Nikkei Asia*, 1 March 2023, https://asia.nikkei.com/Business/Technology/MWC-2023/Huawei-returns-to-global-stage-with-focus-on-5G-and-the-cloud; Dashveenjit Kaur, "Huawei planning its comeback in 5G smartphones", *Techwire Asia*, 13 July 2023, https://techwireasia.com/2023/07/5g-smartphone-will-be-the-comeback-for-huawei/.

[64]   Yifan Yu, "Nvidia revenue hits record $13.5bn amid surging AI demand", *Nikkei Asia*, 24 August 2023, https://asia.nikkei.com/Business/Tech/Semiconductors/Nvidia-revenue-hits-record-13.5bn-amid-surging-AI-demand.

[65]   Arjun Kharpal, "Nvidia warns more semiconductor curbs will end U.S. chipmakers' ability to compete in China", CNBC, 24 August 2023, www.cnbc.com/2023/08/24/nvidia-says-ai-chip-export-curbs-to-china-will-hit-us-chipmakers.html.

[66]   Akito Tanaka and Grace Li, "U.S. big tech won't shake its China addiction", *Nikkei Asia*, 12 July 2023, https://asia.nikkei.com/Spotlight/The-Big-Story/U.S.-big-tech-won-t-shake-its-China-addiction.

of China to avoid complications from the geopolitical tensions between Washington and Beijing. S&P found that China saw a huge decline in US private equity investments in 2022, and Southeast Asia has been one of the prime beneficiaries from that pullback.[67] Malaysia, Thailand, and the Philippines are already part of the global semiconductor value chain with experience in assembly, testing, and packaging. Intel recently announced that it will build a new facility for advanced 3D chip packaging in Malaysia.[68]

However, countries in the region will find it difficult to avoid some of the downsides if US export controls and investment restrictions expand and escalate, resulting in global technological bifurcation. As Foreign Minister Balakrishnan pointed out, the "common stack of science, technology, and supply chains" has served as a global public good driving innovation and prosperity, and its fracture will be "inflationary, disruptive, and dangerous".[69] Thus, it behoves countries in the region to contemplate the construction of an alternative, "non-aligned" technological architecture that is "multipolar, open, and rules-based" in the face of extreme great power competition.[70]

---

[67] Reva Goujon, Charlie Vest, and Thilo Hanemann, *Big Strides in a Small Yard: The New US Outbound Investment Screening Regime*, Rhodium Group Research (New York: Rhodium Group, 2023), https://rhg.com/research/big-strides-in-a-small-yard-the-new-us-outbound-investment-screening-regime/.; Ali Imran Naqvi and Annie Sabater, "China sees huge decline in US private equity investments in 2022", *S&P Global Market Intelligence*, 7 February 2023, www.spglobal.com/marketintelligence/en/news-insights/latest-news-headlines/china-sees-huge-decline-in-us-private-equity-investments-in-2022-74018423.

[68] Cheng Ting-Fang, "Intel to quadruple cutting-edge chip packaging capacity by 2025", *Nikkei Asia*, 23 August 2023, https://asia.nikkei.com/Business/Tech/Semiconductors/Intel-to-quadruple-cutting-edge-chip-packaging-capacity-by-2025.

[69] Singapore Ministry of Foreign Affairs, *Transcript*.

[70] *Ibid.*

CHAPTER 4

ASEAN Digital Transformation and the US–China Technological Competition

Muhammad Faizal and Sarah Teo

Introduction

I f the approaches of the Association of Southeast Asian Nations (ASEAN) and its member states towards the US–China rivalry had to be summed up in one phrase, "Don't make us choose" would certainly be among the top contenders.[1] As Beijing and Washington have expanded and deepened their areas of competition, Southeast Asian capitals have steadfastly repeated the mantra of not wanting to take a side between the major powers. The strategy may differ across the different ASEAN member states in practice and in details, but it is clear that regional countries broadly continue to hedge their bets amidst the vacillations in major power relations. Since the late 2010s, these vacillations have in part been driven by the contest between China and the United States for leadership in trade and technology. Beijing has

---

[1] Jonathan Stromseth, *Don't Make Us Choose: Southeast Asia in the Throes of US–China Rivalry*, Foreign Policy at Brookings, (Washington, D.C.: The Brookings Institution, 2019), www.brookings.edu/articles/dont-make-us-choose-southeast-asia-in-the-throes-of-us-china-rivalry/.

launched initiatives such as the Made in China (MIC) 2025 and the Digital Silk Road (DSR) to boost its dominance in high-tech industries and presence in global technological infrastructure, while Washington has sought to counter China's rising influence in these fields through measures such as banning equipment from Chinese companies, such as Huawei Technologies and ZTE, and working closely with its fellow Quad members on critical and emerging technologies. Self-sufficiency in high-tech manufacturing and the diversification of supply chains have also been prominent themes in the technological rivalry, even as the narrative has moved from "decoupling" to "de-risking". Based on the literature, this rivalry has proceeded along three broad lines: the adoption of technology; the access to raw materials, talent, and equipment for technological development; and the standards and norms governing the use and development of technology.

For ASEAN and its member states, the competition over technology presents both opportunities and challenges. Bearing in mind the absence of a collective ASEAN approach towards the US–China technological rivalry — "Don't make us choose" aside — ASEAN member states have arguably benefitted to some extent from the increased options in capacity-building and cooperation as a consequence of the rivalry but have also had to navigate the complexities of engaging the competing major powers. In essence, the responses of ASEAN member states have been two-pronged. ASEAN member states have rhetorically advocated through diplomatic fora against bifurcation and have emphasised the importance of inclusive digital cooperation; each member state has also concretely adopted digitalisation policies based on considerations such as national development interests, domestic technological capacities, access and affordability of Chinese or Western technological solutions, and the state of their bilateral relations with China and the West.

This chapter is organised as follows. The next section outlines ASEAN's conventional approach towards the major powers to establish the context for the rest of the analysis. The third section examines the key aspects of the technological rivalry, as well as its impact on ASEAN and its member states. This is followed by a discussion of the two-pronged responses of ASEAN member states, before the chapter concludes with a consideration of the implications for ASEAN.

ASEAN and the Major Powers

Notions of inclusive engagement, enmeshment of external partners, and ASEAN centrality have shaped ASEAN's post-Cold War approach towards the major powers. Underlying these principles is an acknowledgement that while the engagement and presence of extra-regional powers are essential for Southeast Asia's peace and stability, the materially weaker Southeast Asian countries could also easily be dominated by those bigger powers. ASEAN has thus had to tread a fine line between cooperating with the extra-regional countries on various agendas relating to Southeast Asia on the one hand and ensure that they do not overly intervene in the region to the extent of overshadowing ASEAN and its member states on the other. ASEAN's approach towards the major and regional powers is exemplified in multilateral platforms such as the ASEAN Regional Forum (ARF), East Asia Summit (EAS), and ASEAN Defence Ministers' Meeting-Plus (ADMM-Plus), as well as in ASEAN's efforts to advance the "ASEAN Plus One" cooperative frameworks with the respective dialogue partners. These platforms reflect ASEAN's pursuit for inclusive engagement that involves all the key regional stakeholders — including countries like Australia, China, Japan, India, and the United States — with ASEAN as the main convenor and agenda-setter of these processes. The dialogue partners are nevertheless offered a stake in the organisation's success through, among other initiatives, co-chairmanship of activities like working groups or joint military exercises. With their relatively diverse membership compositions, it is not surprising that ASEAN-led cooperation often arrives at lowest-common-denominator outcomes that balance among the interests and sensitivities of all participants.

To some extent, individual sets of bilateral relations between ASEAN member states and the major powers may thus be more effective in serving substantive interests or fulfilling specific objectives.[2] Bilateral arrangements allow the parties involved to negotiate and establish agreements in a more straightforward manner, given the narrower range of interests and preferences involved. As we will see, individual ASEAN member states have worked out technology-related agreements with the respective major powers. For ASEAN and its member states, engagement with the major powers is also targeted at capacity-building. ASEAN has significant potential. Recent estimates by the International Monetary Fund (IMF) indicate that Southeast Asia will be the fastest growing region, with Vietnam in the lead, while other projections forecast that ASEAN is poised to become the world's fourth-largest economy by 2030.[3] Southeast Asia is also the fastest growing Internet

---

[2] See N. Ganesan and Ramses Amer, *International Relations in Southeast Asia: Between Bilateralism and Multilateralism* (Singapore: ISEAS Publishing, 2010), pp. 328–330; Ken Heydon, "The rise of bilateralism: implications for ASEAN, and beyond", *East Asia Forum*, 1 February 2010, www.eastasiaforum.org/2010/02/01/the-rise-of-bilateralism-implications-for-asean-and-beyond/.

[3] Center for Strategic and International Studies, "The latest on Southeast Asia: 27 October 2022", *CSIS Blog*, 27 October 2022, www.csis.org/blogs/latest-southeast-asia/latest-southeast-asia-october-27-2022; Joo-Ok Lee and Shaun Adam, "ASEAN is poised for post-pandemic inclusive growth and prosperity — Here's why", *World Economic Forum*, 18 January 2022, www.weforum.org/agenda/2022/01/asean-is-poised-for-post-pandemic-inclusive-growth-and-prosperity-heres-why/; Jayant Menon, "Southeast Asian Economies: Out of the storm, clouds on the horizon", *Fulcrum*, 20 February 2023, https://fulcrum.sg/southeast-asian-economies-out-of-the-storm-clouds-on-the-horizon/.

market in the world.[4] These indicate that ASEAN and its member states already have a rather solid base upon which they could further their development.

To maximise this potential, however, regional infrastructure and connectivity would need to be strengthened. ASEAN has already embarked on such programmes, including those as listed in the Master Plan on ASEAN Connectivity (MPAC) 2025, ASEAN Economic Community Blueprint 2025, and ASEAN Digital Masterplan (ADM) 2025. The MPAC 2025 aims to strengthen physical, institutional, and people-to-people connectivity across Southeast Asia, while the ADM 2025 envisions the innovation of new technologies and services, the reduction of regulatory barriers, and "high quality and ubiquitous connectivity throughout ASEAN".[5] Dialogue partners have also committed to cooperation in the items identified in these plans. At the ASEAN–US Special Summit in 2022, for example, Washington pledged to offer capacity-building assistance for ASEAN and Southeast Asian countries in areas like maritime infrastructure and healthcare.[6] Meanwhile, Beijing has agreed to provide support for the Southeast Asian grouping on healthcare, trade matters, and disaster management.[7]

---

[4] *World Economic Forum*, "Digital ASEAN", *World Economic Forum*, accessed 4 August 2023, www.weforum.org/projects/digital-asean.

[5] ASEAN, *Masterplan for ASEAN Connectivity 2025*, (Jakarta, Indonesia: Association of Southeast Asian Nations, 2017), pp. 1–122, https://asean.org/wp-content/uploads/2018/01/47.-December-2017-MPAC2025-2nd-Reprint-.pdf; ASEAN, *ASEAN Digital Masterplan 2025*, (Jakarta, Indonesia: Association of Southeast Asian Nations, 2021), 5, https://asean.org/wp-content/uploads/2021/08/ASEAN-Digital-Masterplan-2025.pdf.

[6] The White House, Fact sheet: US–ASEAN special summit in Washington, DC, 12 May 2022, www.whitehouse.gov/briefing-room/statements-releases/2022/05/12/fact-sheet-u-s-asean-special-summit-in-washington-dc/.

[7] ASEAN, Plan of action to implement the ASEAN–China strategic partnership for peace and prosperity (2021–2025), (Bali, Indonesia: Association of Southeast Asian Nations, 2021), pp. 1–28, https://asean.org/wp-content/uploads/2022/08/ASEAN-China-POA-2021-2025_Updated-with-ANNEX.pdf.

Chinese companies have also helped to build high-speed railways in Indonesia and Laos. It is clear that there are benefits from engaging with the major powers.

For these reasons, ASEAN and its member states actively avoid "choosing" between China and the United States. Even as the major power rivalry has intensified through the 2010s and into the early 2020s, Southeast Asian countries have tried to remain on constructive terms with both sides and avoid getting caught in the crossfire. To be sure, the "middle ground" differs for each country depending on various factors, including whether they have any existing disputes with China or the United States, the government of the day, domestic politicking, or the extent of their trade or security interdependence with either power. In this context, the strategies that ASEAN and its member states have adopted towards China and the United States may vary, but they remain within the limited confines established by the desire not to choose sides. The strategies would also be driven by capacity-building goals and the need to ensure that the regional environment remains stable for socio-economic development. As we will see, these considerations are illustrative of the approaches by ASEAN and its member states towards the US–China technological competition.

US–China Technological Competition and Impact on ASEAN

The origins of the US–China technological rivalry can be traced to 2015, when two key developments occurred. First, China released the MIC 2025 strategy, outlining its transformation "into a leading manufacturing power ... in line with the rapid advances in science and technology" by 2049.[8] Second, China introduced the DSR as a component of the Belt and Road Initiative (BRI). The DSR aims specifically for three main goals: to strengthen regional and international connectivity; to upgrade traditional industries and employment in BRI countries "by opening up China's market with China's digital assets"; and to form a regional community led by China based on common economic interests.[9] The DSR and the MIC 2025 alarmed some in Washington, and the then-new-President Donald Trump sought action against China for what was perceived as unfair trade practices and the theft of intellectual property. Concerns about the rising technological dominance of Chinese companies culminated, among other things, in US sanctions against Huawei and the eventual coalescence of a technological war between Beijing and Washington.

The literature generally identifies three key points of contention between both sides in the technological rivalry — the adoption of technology; the access to raw materials, talent, and equipment for technological development; and the standards and norms governing the use and development of technology. These also have had implications for relations between ASEAN and the two major powers.

First, the US–China technological competition involves a race for the adoption of technology. It is not so much about the access to new technology itself, but more about "the ability to 'get there first'".[10]

---

[8] The State Council of the People's Republic of China, State Council Information Office, "Made in China 2025" plan issued, 19 May 2015, http://english.www.gov.cn/policies/latest_releases/2015/05/19/content_281475110703534.htm.

[9] Brigitte Dekker, Maaike Okano-Heijmans, and Eric Siyi Zhang, *Unpacking China's Digital Silk Road*, Clingendael Report (The Netherlands: Clingendael Institute, 2020), p. 4, www.clingendael.org/sites/default/files/2020-07/Report_Digital_Silk_Road_July_2020.pdf.

[10] Amy J. Nelson cited in Ryan Hass *et al.*, *US-China Technology Competition. A Brookings Global China Interview*, Global China: Assessing China's Growing Role in the World, (Washington, D.C.: The Brookings Institution, 2021), www.brookings.edu/articles/u-s-china-technology-competition/.

The United States is potentially losing its edge as the global leader in science and technology as China has already emerged as the leading player in several areas like 5G, e-commerce, and fintech, and is narrowing the gap with the US in others.[11] For instance, while Washington may remain the front-runner in AI given its current superiority in hardware development and research talent, China "has a massive trove of the AI-ready data that fuels technological development, and a strong political will to succeed".[12] In 2017, China's State Council released the "Next Generation Artificial Intelligence Development Plan" which outlined aspirations for China to become a "global AI innovation center" by 2030.[13] Considering the implications for global military and economic primacy, such developments have been viewed with unease by Washington, which has culminated in its response of preventing US firms from exporting advanced technology to China.

ASEAN and its member states have regarded the techno-nationalism with some anxiety in the context of the broader rivalry between the two major powers for global leadership. The competing visions of techno-nationalism put forward by China and the United States could result in Southeast Asian countries "[having] to navigate a complex digital

---

[11] Graham Allison *et al.*, *The Great Tech Rivalry: China vs the U.S.*, (Cambridge, MA: Belfer Center for Science and International Affairs, 2021), 2, www.belfercenter.org/sites/default/files/GreatTechRivalry_ChinavsUS_211207.pdf; Lurong Chen, *Digital Asia: Facing Challenges from GVCs Digitalisation, US–China Decoupling, and the Covid-19 Pandemic* (Jakarta, Indonesia: Economic Research Institute for ASEAN and East Asia, 2021), p. 3, www.eria.org/uploads/media/policy-brief/Digital-Asia-Facing-Challenges-from-GVC-Digitalisation-US-China-Decoupling.pdf.

[12] Jun-E. Tan, "What does the US-China AI rivalry mean for Southeast Asia?" *The Diplomat*, 7 February 2022, https://thediplomat.com/2022/02/what-does-the-us-china-ai-rivalry-mean-for-southeast-asia/.

[13] Department of International Cooperation, Ministry of Science and Technology, P. R. China, "Next generation artificial intelligence development plan issued by state council", *China Science and Technology Newsletter* no. 17, 15 September 2017, p. 4, http://fi.china-embassy.gov.cn/eng/kxjs/201710/P020210628714286134479.pdf.

fracture resulting from technological bifurcation".[14] The exclusive nature of such cooperation, moreover, would be in opposition to ASEAN's typical approach of inclusive engagement — which is not only the grouping's *raison d'etre* in the regional multilateral architecture but also a strategy that has enabled it to remain as the hub of regional multilateralism. Based on current developments, ASEAN may also find it difficult to continue its focus on pragmatic economic considerations over geopolitics.[15] In other words, the effectiveness of ASEAN's longstanding formula to maintain its relevance may eventually be eroded.

The second aspect of the technological rivalry is about the access to raw materials, talent, and equipment for technological development. When framed in the context of national security, the US restrictions on chip exports to China and China's export controls on rare earth resources to the United States are clear examples of the dynamics at play. Partnerships are also an important element in this context. Washington has urged its allies to follow its restrictions on exporting semiconductors to China, with a "Chip 4 alliance", involving Japan, South Korea, Taiwan, and the United States, seemingly taking shape — albeit with some limitations given the close economic relations between some of these countries and China. At the urging of the United States and in the interest of national security, the Netherlands implemented new controls on 1 September 2023 that could limit the export of advanced chipmaking equipment to Chinese companies.[16] Both China and the

---

[14] Muhammad Faizal and Dymples Leong. 2020. "Impact of US-China technationalism on ASEAN", *The ASEAN Post*, 7 November 2020, https://theaseanpost.com/article/impact-us-china-technationalism-asean.

[15] Shashi Jayakumar and Manoj Harjani, "Between byte and bark — Singapore, US and Chinese tech", *Today Online*, 21 October 2020, www.todayonline.com/commentary/between-byte-and-bark-singapore-us-and-chinese-tech.

[16] *The Straits Times*, "ASML hit with new limits on chip gear exports to China", 30 June 2023, *The Straits Times*, www.straitstimes.com/business/asml-hit-with-new-limits-on-chip-gear-exports-to-china.

United States have embarked on efforts to diversify supply chains of raw materials and critical minerals, and to boost their respective self-sufficiencies. This has given rise to the phenomenon of "friendshoring", which involves the rerouting of supply chains to "countries regarded as political and economic allies".[17] In the longer term, friendshoring may result in greater fragmentation of the global economy and geopolitics.[18]

To be sure, some ASEAN member states have benefitted from the rerouting and diversification of supply chains. Vietnam has reportedly been "the biggest winner" from the redirection of supply chains and economic links from China to Southeast Asia, while Indonesia has drawn investments from Chinese mining companies in its nickel industry.[19] In an interview in April 2023, Malaysia's Minister of Investment, Trade, and Industry Tengku Zafrul Aziz highlighted the potential gains for the country from US-led friendshoring in the short term, although he also cautioned that a sustained decoupling between China and the US would damage the global economy.[20] Similarly, as business owners and observers have pointed out, the relocation of

---

[17] Stefan Ellerbeck, "What's the difference between 'friendshoring' and other global trade buzzwords?", *World Economic Forum*, 17 February 2023, www.weforum.org/agenda/2023/02/friendshoring-global-trade-buzzwords/.

[18] Ellerbeck, "What's the difference?"

[19] Ann Marie Murphy, *Southeast Asia Amidst US-China Economic Competition*, Perry World House, (Philadelphia, PA: University of Pennsylvania, 2023), https://global.upenn.edu/perryworldhouse/news/southeast-asia-amidst-us-china-economic-competition; see also Yudith Ho and Eko Listiyorini, "Chinese companies are flocking to Indonesia for Its nickel", *Bloomberg*, 16 December 2022, www.bloomberg.com/news/articles/2022-12-15/chinese-companies-are-flocking-to-indonesia-for-its-nickel.

[20] Bhavan Jaipragas, "Western friendshoring benefits Malaysia amid US–China rivalry, but could hurt global economy: trade minister", *South China Morning Post*, 3 April 2023, www.scmp.com/week-asia/economics/article/3215653/western-friendshoring-benefits-malaysia-amid-us-china-rivalry-could-hurt-global-economy-trade.

production facilities to Vietnam is a complex and difficult endeavour.[21] In some ways, the US–China competition over access to raw materials and the resilience of supply chains have thus been to the advantage of several ASEAN member states. Yet, given that the technological rivalry is merely one aspect of the overall US–China competition, greater instability and uncertainty in regional geopolitics may negate the short-term gains enjoyed by some ASEAN member states.

The third aspect of the US–China technological rivalry is the competition for leadership in standards and norm-setting. For a rising power like China, emerging areas such as cybersecurity and AI present opportunities for it "to shape the future of technological development and commercial hierarchies in an enduring fashion" and provide "an alternative model to global governance".[22] To augment its influence, China has proactively participated in international standardising organisations, and it has also proposed norms and rules to govern cyberspace and data security.[23] Initiatives such as the DSR facilitate

---

[21]   Liu Liu, "Shifting supply chains from China to Southeast Asia is hard but necessary", *ThinkChina*, 21 June 2021, www.thinkchina.sg/shifting-supply-chains-china-southeast-asia-hard-necessary.

[22]   Emily de La Bruyère, "Setting the standards locking in China's technological influence", *China's Digital Ambitions: A Global Strategy to Supplant the Liberal Order*, NBR Special Report No. 97 (Seattle: The National Bureau of Asian Research, 2022), pp. 51–52, www.nbr.org/publication/setting-the-standards-locking-in-chinas-technological-influence/; Elina Noor, *Southeast Asia and the China-US Fight for Tech Supremacy*, Asia Global Online, (Hong Kong: Asia Global Institute, The University of Hong Kong, 2023), www.asiaglobalonline.hku.hk/southeast-asia-and-china-us-fight-tech-supremacy.

[23]   Dai Mochinaga, "The Digital Silk Road and China's technology influence in Southeast Asia", *Asia Unbound*, Council on Foreign Relations, 10 June 2021, pp. 7–8, www.cfr.org/sites/default/files/pdf/mochinaga_the-digital-silk-road-and-chinas-technology-influence-in-southeast-asia_june-2021.pdf; The State Council of the People's Republic of China, State Council Information Office, "White paper: Jointly build a community with a shared future in cyberspace", 7 November 2022, http://english.scio.gov.cn/node_8033411.html; Shannon Tiezzi, "China's bid to write the global rules on data security", *The Diplomat*, 10 September 2020, https://thediplomat.com/2020/09/chinas-bid-to-write-the-global-rules-on-data-security/.

Beijing's efforts to establish and harmonise digital standards and norms across countries. The United States, in turn, has launched the Digital Connectivity and Cybersecurity Partnership (DCCP) to support global digital infrastructure-building efforts. Through the DCCP, Washington aims to promote an "open" and "secure" Internet, and advance "resilient and democratic societies" — in contrast to what it perceives as the lack of transparency and accountability in Beijing's digital initiatives.[24]

When it comes to ASEAN, digital standards and norm-setting are likewise varied as regulatory frameworks differ across member states.[25] The fragmentation is likely to deepen as governments and businesses within ASEAN adopt the diverging technological options offered by the major powers, which would also entail buying into their respective technical standards and norms. For example, Huawei's extensive assistance for Laos's infrastructure-building not only suggests that the country "will be locked in to Chinese technologies for decades" but has also "[raised] questions about data privacy given Chinese information and communications technology (ICT) laws".[26] It may be worth noting that from the perspective of Southeast Asian countries — all of whom would be familiar with the unilateral and coercive tendencies of major powers

---

[24] U.S. Department of State, Digital connectivity and cybersecurity partnership, accessed 5 August 2023, www.state.gov/digital-connectivity-and-cybersecurity-partnership/; Chris Meserole cited in Hass et al., (2021), op. cit.

[25] Sithanonxay Suvannaphakdy, "Fragmented digital regulations are constraining ASEAN's digital economy", Fulcrum, 17 February 2023, https://fulcrum.sg/fragmented-digital-regulations-are-constraining-aseans-digital-economy/.

[26] Mochinaga, "The Digital Silk Road", 4; Daniel F. Runde, Romina Bandura, and Rachel Lee, Digitalizing Laos: Improving Government Transparency, the Business Environment, and Human Capital, CSIS Brief, (Washington, D.C.: Center for Strategic and International Studies, 2022), www.csis.org/analysis/digitalizing-laos-improving-government-transparency-business-environment-and-human-capital.

as a whole — neither the Chinese framework nor US framework "is ... morally or ideologically superior to the other".[27] Instead, the challenge for ASEAN and its member states would centre more on ensuring the harmonisation of digital standards and regulations that would smoothen cross-border transactions for businesses in the region.

Following this discussion of the key aspects in the US–China technological rivalry and the impact on ASEAN and its member states, the remaining sections focus on the latter's responses and consider the implications of these responses for ASEAN's institutional dynamics.

Responses of ASEAN Member States to the US–China Technological Competition

The lack of strategic trust amidst geopolitical tensions, US–China technological competition, and the absence of guardrails to keep this competition healthy threaten to hinder the digital ambitions of ASEAN. Moreover, the political and social impact on ASEAN could be disruptive if China and the United States persist on the path of weaponisation of technology and resort to imposing sanctions that affect each other's technological companies and interests in Southeast Asia. The responses of ASEAN member states towards the technological rivalry have been two-pronged. In rhetoric, some ASEAN member states have responded through diplomatic fora to address common concerns. In concrete terms, each member state has also adopted digitalisation policies that focus on national priorities instead of acquiescing to geopolitical pressures. Due to its non-interference principle, ASEAN as an intergovernmental organisation does not advocate a collective stance

---

27   Elina Noor, (2023), *Op. cit.*

regarding the securitisation of critical digital technologies, unlike the European Union (EU), which is a supranational organisation.[28]

At various diplomatic fora, leaders from several ASEAN member states have raised concerns over the impact of US–China technological competition, both as a cautionary note to businesses and people in Southeast Asia and as an appeal to China and the United States to manage their competition responsibly. These ASEAN leaders expressed concerns that geopolitical considerations increasingly overshadow economic imperatives underpinning sound trade and technological policies.

For example, Singaporean Minister for Foreign Affairs Vivian Balakrishnan spoke about techno-nationalism during the second Next Step Global Conference in November 2022, where he made several key points.[29] First, he stated that Washington and Beijing have been making policy decisions and implementing countermeasures to outplay each other in the technological competition, but these actions could affect ASEAN. Second, he noted a bifurcation of technological standards would not only disrupt global systems that have enabled prosperity, peace, and stability since the end of World War 2 but would also make technological products more costly and result in inflationary pressures. Third, he suggested that the rest of the world that refuses to choose sides could "conceive a world in which we can have a more open, inclusive, multilateral network of science, technology, and supply

---

28 Jakob Hanke Vela and Barbara Moens, "EU looks to ban companies from making sensitive tech in China", *Politico*, 20 June 2023, www.politico.eu/article/eu-ban-companies-make-sensitive-tech-china/.

29 Singapore Ministry of Foreign Affairs, Transcript of minister for foreign affairs Dr Vivian Balakrishnan's remarks at the 2nd next step global conference 2022 at Raffles Hotel on 9 November 2022, 10 November 2022, www.mfa.gov.sg/Newsroom/Press-Statements-Transcripts-and-Photos/2022/11/221110nextstep.

chains".[30] He elucidated that this network has to be "multipolar, open, and rules-based", similar to the Non-Aligned Movement (NAM) that came about during the Cold War to "counterbalance the rapid bipolarisation of the globe".

Malaysian Prime Minister Anwar Ibrahim spoke about technological competition during the Boao Forum for Asia in March 2023, where he suggested that this issue should be discussed at the highest levels, comparable to economic and security matters.[31] He said that the race for technological superiority "could take a productive or destructive turn" and that "unfettered competition must give way to spirited collaboration". To that end, he emphasised that there should be guardrails to ensure that technological competition would not result in a bifurcated world where costs spiral and progress faces impediments.

Indonesian President Joko Widodo raised important points in 2022 when Indonesia held the presidency of the Group of 20 (G20). During the G20 Leaders' Summit in November 2022, he, as the host, emphasised to the G20 leaders that they should not allow the world to fragment into geopolitical blocs and cause another Cold War to happen.[32] Although his remarks did not specifically mention the US–China technological competition, they broadly reflect the current heightened state of geopolitical tensions of which technological competition plays a part.

---

[30] *Ibid.*

[31] Bernama, "At Boao Forum for Asia, Anwar calls for focus on tech competition, collaboration", *New Straits Times*, 30 March 2023, www.nst.com.my/news/nation/2023/03/894524/boao-forum-asia-anwar-calls-focus-tech-competition-collaboration.

[32] Kiki Siregar, "We must not allow the world to fall into another Cold War: Indonesia's Jokowi at G20 summit", *Channel NewsAsia*, 15 November 2022, www.channelnewsasia.com/asia/g20-bali-indonesia-jokowi-must-not-allow-world-fall-another-cold-war-3072656.

Furthermore, he promoted digital transformation as the key to a better future for people, and stated that this effort requires countries to cooperate in three primary areas.[33] First, he noted that all countries must ensure equal digital access. Second, he stated that the G20 should help developing countries increase digital capacity and its people to develop digital literacy. Third, he urged the G20 countries to develop a safe digital environment, with trust in the digital sector underpinned by global digital governance. He suggested that these conditions for a future digital economy will not be attainable if there is a widening split along geopolitical lines in the technological domain.

Concerning digitalisation policies, this analysis focuses on the adoption of 5G technology, a foundational enabler of the digital economy and critical information infrastructure. 5G technology remains a priority in ASEAN's digitalisation plans and is one of the primary areas of contention between China and the United States. 5G technology has been at the crux of risks relating to malicious cyber activities and the ideological contest between China and the United States on digital authoritarianism versus a free and open digital commons. Countries in the Quad have imposed barriers to thwart Chinese technological companies from participating in their national 5G networks and have advocated Open Radio Access Networks (Open RAN) as a novel alternative to the more mature traditional RAN technology that Chinese companies offer.[34] The United States and the EU are hardening their stance to "rip and replace" Huawei and ZTE

---

[33] Cabinet Secretariat of the Republic of Indonesia, President Jokowi highlight three points to accelerate digital transformation, 16 November 2022, https://setkab.go.id/en/president-jokowi-highlight-three-points-to-accelerate-digital-transformation/.

[34] Alexandra Seymour and Martjin Rasser, *Better Together: How the Quad Countries Can Operationalise 5G Security*, CDN Series, (India: Chrome Dot Network, Observer Research Foundation, 2022), www.orfonline.org/research/how-the-quad-countries-can-operationalise-5g-security/.

hardware from existing 5G networks. However, this policy comes with great costs, and relations with China would take an adversarial turn.[35] The West has also undertaken diplomatic research efforts to raise warning flags about the risks of emerging economies, including those in Southeast Asia, allowing Huawei equipment in their national 5G networks.[36]

In being politically neutral and economically pragmatic, ASEAN member states have adopted varying policies on 5G based on a quadrumvirate of factors, viz., national development interests, domestic technological capacities, access and affordability of Chinese or Western technological solutions, and the state of their bilateral relations with China and the West.

On one end of the spectrum, developing ASEAN member states — particularly Cambodia, Laos, and Myanmar — that have traditionally closer defence, economic, and political relations with China (and Russia) leverage Chinese technological solutions more as these serve their national interests better. First, there is better access to Chinese technological solutions as Chinese companies such as Huawei and Hikvision have established a longer market presence in developing countries, including those in the ASEAN region. These companies are more willing to conduct business with developing

---

[35] Jon Gold, "EU's changing stance on Huawei could impact 5G networks already in place", *Network World*, 8 May 2023, www.networkworld.com/article/3695730/eus-changing-stance-on-huawei-could-impact-5g-networks-already-in-place.html.

[36] *Reuters*, "EU, US warn Malaysia of security risk in Huawei's bid for 5G role, Financial Times reports", *Reuters*, 2 May 2023, www.reuters.com/technology/eu-us-warn-malaysia-national-security-risk-huaweis-bid-5g-role-ft-2023-05-02/; Dirk van der Kley, Benjamin Herscovitch, and Gatra Priyandita, "China Inc. and Indonesia's technology future", *Policy Options Paper* no. 27, (Canberra, Australia: Australian National University, National Security College, 2022), pp. 1–4, https://nsc.crawford.anu.edu.au/sites/default/files/publication/nsc_crawford_anu_edu_au/2022-07/web_nsc_pop_indonesia_education_no.27_1.pdf.

countries that are emerging markets but deemed by Western companies as less profitable.[37] Second, Chinese technological solutions are not only highly advanced but also more affordable than Western ones. Performance and cost issues are paramount considerations for developing countries.[38] Third, Chinese companies, especially Huawei, have been partnering with governments of developing countries in technological talent development, innovation, and cybersecurity capacity-building. These efforts aim to help developing countries achieve their national development goals through the digitalisation of their economies. Fourth, China has been more politically supportive of governments in developing ASEAN countries. On the contrary, Western largesse often comes with preconditions to meet standards of human rights, free speech, and fair elections, and involves not using Western digital technologies in a manner that is inconsistent with these principles.

For example, Laos has been a significant beneficiary of Chinese business and infrastructural investments. Since 2008, Huawei has been developing local technological talent in Laos through its "Seeds for the Future" programme. In its national effort to boost infrastructural capacity and turn itself from a landlocked to a land-linked country, Laos has depended on Huawei to build its national 5G network, and the company serves 75% of its population. Huawei's 5G technological solutions power data communications, cloud computing, the Internet-of-Things (IoT), and the security management system of the

---

[37] Tabatha T. Anderson, "The developing world needs an alternative to Chinese tech", *Pacific Forum*, 22 August 2023, https://pacforum.org/publication/pacnet-65-the-developing-world-needs-an-alternative-to-chinese-tech.

[38] Shaun Turton and Tomoya Onishi, "Cambodia 5G set to leapfrog ASEAN rivals with Huawei and ZTE", *Nikkei Asia*, 5 September 2019, https://asia.nikkei.com/Spotlight/5G-networks/Cambodia-5G-set-to-leapfrog-ASEAN-rivals-with-Huawei-and-ZTE.

Vientiane–Vangvieng expressway.[39] This road infrastructure is the first smart expressway in Laos and was built jointly by the Lao government and the Chinese company Yunnan Construction and Investment Holding Group (YCIH).[40] The China–Laos railway, which is the first modern railway in Laos, connects its capital, Vientiane, to Kunming in southern China and is powered by Huawei's 5G technological solutions.[41] Despite the significant technological and economic influence that China has over Laos, the latter has taken care not to choose sides. Laos aims to balance its interests by engaging with other international partners, such as Thailand and Vietnam, to increase its policy options in the areas of trade, diplomacy, and defence.[42]

On the other end of the spectrum are more technologically developed ASEAN member states, particularly Vietnam, which is reportedly among the top 10 countries with the most developed 5G networks.[43] While Vietnam has not explicitly banned Chinese technological companies from participating in its 5G networks, its telecommunications service providers have avoided using Chinese

39   Chris Devonshire Ellis, "2023 foreign investment opportunities in Laos", *ASEAN Briefing*, 26 July 2022, www.aseanbriefing.com/news/2023-foreign-investment-opportunities-in-laos/.

40   Huaxia, "Huawei helps build 1st smart expressway in Laos", *Xinhuanet*, 22 December 2020, www.xinhuanet.com/english/2020-12/22/c_139609360.htm.

41   *Khmer Times*, "Huawei smart railway solution and 5G network supports the Laos-China Railway grand launching", *Khmer Times*, 4 December 2021, www.khmertimeskh.com/50982614/huawei-smart-railway-solution-and-5g-network-supports-the-laos-china-railway-grand-launching/.

42   Joanne Lin, "Changing perceptions in Laos toward China", *ISEAS Perspective* no. 55, 17 July 2023, www.iseas.edu.sg/posts/2023-55-changing-perceptions-in-laos-toward-china-by-joanne-lin/.

43   Son Nguyen, "5G to boost Vietnam's growth", *Hanoi Times*, 8 January 2023, https://hanoitimes.vn/5g-technology-to-boost-vietnams-growth-322759.html.

hardware.[44] Vietnam's telecommunications companies are developing indigenous 5G technologies and partnering with European (Nokia) and South Korean (Samsung) companies to roll out 5G networks. The absence of Chinese hardware in Vietnam's 5G networks is due in part to the significant security challenge that China poses to Vietnam.[45] Chinese-linked actors had conducted disruptive cyber attacks, relating to the South China Sea dispute, on Vietnam's airports and national carriers in 2013 and 2016.[46] Still, avoidance instead of a Western-style ban on Chinese 5G technologies is Vietnam's unique digital security policy approach that steers clear of an alliance with the United States while maintaining a good neighbour policy with China.

Singapore has taken the middle path in the rollout of its national 5G networks by allowing telecommunications companies to bid for 5G licences regardless of whether they partner with Huawei, Ericsson, or Nokia. Telecommunications company TPG, which partnered with Huawei, was unsuccessful in its bid to participate in building Singapore's national 5G networks, but this was not the result of America's campaign against Huawei. Rather, the bid evaluation was informed by commercial factors and the government's technical standards on performance, security, and resilience.[47] Telecommunication companies can use Huawei hardware for small-scale or localised 5G networks. Nonetheless,

---

[44] David Sacks, "China's Huawei is winning the 5G race. Here's what the United States should do to respond", Council on Foreign Relations, 29 March 2021, www.cfr.org/blog/china-huawei-5g.

[45] Le Hong Hiep, "Why does Vietnam shy away from Huawei's 5G technologies?" *Fulcrum*, 2 May 2019, https://fulcrum.sg/why-does-vietnam-shy-away-from-huaweis-5g-technologies-by-le-hong-hiep/.

[46] *Viet Nam News*, "Chinese hackers attack VN's airports and Vietnam Airlines' website", *Viet Nam News*, 29 July 2016, https://vietnamnews.vn/society/300416/chinese-hackers-attack-vns-airports-and-vietnam-airlines-website.html.

[47] Amalina Anuar, "5G in Singapore — Is the tide turning against Huawei?", *Today Online*, 12 August 2020, www.todayonline.com/commentary/5g-singapore-tide-turning-against-huawei.

"limiting Huawei to non-core elements of 5G networks may be a strategic step for Singapore", not due to strategic alignment with the United States, but to "pre-empt plausible supply chain disruptions to national infrastructure if the US effectively severs Huawei's global access to semiconductors".[48] Indirectly, this step provides some assurance to the United States, with whom Singapore maintains a strategic partnership to promote regional stability, access state-of-the-art military hardware, and enhance cybersecurity cooperation in the civilian and military sectors.[49]

Barring the outbreak of a hot war in the Indo-Pacific that would disrupt supply chains, it is foreseeable that ASEAN member states would continue their digitalisation policies based on the principles of political neutrality and economic pragmatism while concomitantly leveraging diplomatic fora to dissuade China and the United States from weaponising their influence over technology. While Western powers would continue sounding warnings about cybersecurity threats, trust issues, and foreign interference relating to Chinese technologies, countries may have similar concerns over Western technologies. Since 2022, several Western technological companies have aligned with Western sanctions, making use of their influence and market power to digitally isolate Russia after it invaded Ukraine.[50] This unprecedented

---

48   Muhammad Faizal Abdul Rahman, "Singapore decides on 5G networks: Is Huawei banned?", *The Diplomat*, 2 July 2020, https://thediplomat.com/2020/07/singapore-decides-on-5g-networks-is-huawei-banned/.

49   Aqil Haziq Mahmud, "More cybersecurity cooperation between Singapore, US in public, defence and financial sectors", *Channel NewsAsia*, 23 August 2021, www.channelnewsasia.com/singapore/singapore-us-mou-cybersecurity-cooperation-public-defence-finance-2130121; Mercedes Ruehl, "Singapore deepens US defence ties despite Chinese financial inflows", *Financial Times*, 30 April 2023, www.ft.com/content/0c20823d-2d5f-435e-aec4-269dbe5dafb4.

50   Dashveenjit Kaur, "Here's the technology companies severing ties with Russia", *TechHQ*, 2 March 2022, https://techhq.com/2022/03/heres-the-technology-companies-severing-ties-with-russia/.

development raised the possibility of future scenarios where Western technological sanctions could be applied against countries that prioritise their own strategic interests, which may not be aligned with the interests of Western powers during a conflict. In a similar light, ASEAN witnessed how Western powers cut off Russian banks from the SWIFT global financial messaging network as a strategic tool to coerce Russia into ending its invasion of Ukraine. This game-changing development has stimulated interest among ASEAN member states to explore alternative financial systems — such as China's Cross-Border Interbank Payment System (CIPS) — as a pragmatic move to preserve neutrality and increase their options in this area as a safeguard amidst rising geopolitical tensions.[51] The preponderance of power in the global digital commons, competing visions of digital governance, strained relations between the major powers limiting progress on the implementation of international cyber norms, and other states' aversion to tech-related sanctions may reaffirm ASEAN member states' choice of non-alignment in the technological competition and putting their national interests first.

Conclusion

As long as the geopolitical situation permits, ASEAN and its member states will likely maintain the mantra of "Don't make us choose" and observe economic pragmatism in response to the US–China technological competition. Focusing on socio-economic development and less contentious issues would drive member states to invest more

---

[51] Robert Greene, *Southeast Asia's Growing Interest in Non-dollar Financial Channels — and the Renminbi's Potential Role*, (Washington, D.C.: Carnegie Endowment for International Peace, 2022), https://carnegieendowment.org/2022/08/22/southeast-asia-s-growing-interest-in-non-dollar-financial-channels-and-renminbi-s-potential-role-pub-87731.

efforts in harmonising digital standards and regulations, such as the new regional guidelines on AI and the proposed ASEAN Digital Economy Framework Agreement (ASEAN DEFA).

Member states will capitalise on opportunities from the technological competition to serve their respective economic interests where possible. Vietnam aims to benefit from the redirection of supply chains, such as in the production of smartphones, from China to Southeast Asia.[52] Malaysia is a potentially suitable location to set up semiconductor facilities for Taiwanese technological companies aiming to mitigate the risks of US–China rivalry.[53] Indonesia aims to benefit from investments in its nickel industry, which is crucial to the production of batteries for electric vehicles — another potential area of US–China technological competition.[54] Malaysia, Singapore, Thailand, and Vietnam are vying with each other to be neutral hubs for Chinese and Western data centres.[55] Singapore's position as a neutral hub for Chinese and Western data centres (for example, China Mobile and Google) and submarine data cables (for example, SEA Cable Exchange by Huawei and Echo by Meta and Google) not only serves its economic interests but could also arguably promote a "balance of power" in ASEAN's digital domain by ensuring that neither China nor the United States dominates the global digital commons that the region needs for its digital ambitions.

---

[52] Lam Du, "Why Apple and Xiaomi moved production to Vietnam", *Vietnamnet Global*, 17 November 2022, https://vietnamnet.vn/en/why-apple-and-xiaomi-moved-production-to-vietnam-2080708.html.

[53] Asila Jalil, "US–China rift spells opportunity for Taiwanese tech firms to explore Malaysia", *New Straits Times*, 10 November 2022, www.nst.com.my/business/2022/11/849148/us-china-rift-spells-opportunity-taiwanese-tech-firms-explore-malaysia.

[54] EIU, "US–China tensions: Are EVs next in the firing line?", *The Economist Intelligence Unit*, 7 July 2023, www.eiu.com/n/us-china-tensions-are-evs-next-in-the-firing-line/.

[55] *The Straits Times*, "Malaysia woos Microsoft, Google to bolster data hub ambitions", *The Straits Times*, 12 June 2023, www.straitstimes.com/asia/se-asia/malaysia-woos-microsoft-google-to-bolster-data-hub-ambitions.

Still, the political neutrality of ASEAN in technological competition may not be sustainable if a hot war breaks out in the Indo-Pacific. This may create severe disruptions to the digital supply chain, including cyber operations that exploit 5G network vulnerabilities, and push technological companies from opposing sides of the war to the frontlines, as witnessed in the war between Russia and Ukraine. Furthermore, the sabotage of submarine telegraph cables by warring navies during the two World Wars could be a bellwether of hybrid warfare targeting submarine data cables if a hot war breaks out, disrupting digital connectivity in Southeast Asia. It is uncertain what ASEAN's fallback position on cyber resilience for critical information infrastructure would be in a war scenario as it is not stated in the ASEAN Cybersecurity Cooperation Strategy 2021–2025. For example, the strategy states that information sharing and incident response are among the six pillars of the ASEAN Critical Information Infrastructure Protection Framework. However, member states that use more indigenous or Western 5G technologies may baulk at sharing cyber threat intelligence with those who depend more on Chinese technologies, and vice versa. Another example is the "ASEAN Guidelines for Strengthening Resilience and Repair of Submarine Cables" that ASEAN released in 2019 to complement the ASEAN ICT Masterplan 2020. It is uncertain if these guidelines are sufficient to safeguard digital connectivity in the ASEAN in a war scenario between the major powers. Furthermore, an evolving war situation could push countries to shift from political neutrality to alignment if they assess that their national (and economic) interests are in jeopardy, as seen in the case of Finland and Sweden. Ultimately, the confluence of competing national interests and unchecked US–China tensions could make technological competition the next stress point that erodes ASEAN cohesion and centrality.

Printed in the United States
by Baker & Taylor Publisher Services